Daniel and his Visions

The message of Daniel chapters 7-12

Steve Wilmshurst

The quotations from 1 Maccabees are from the New Revised Standard Version Bible: Anglicized Edition, copyright © 1989, 1995 National Council of the Churches of Christ in the United States of America. Used by permission. All rights reserved.

ISBN: 978-1-97703-591-2

Contents

Preface   ii

Introduction   1

Summary of chapters 1-6   12

Daniel 7: The beasts defeated   22

Daniel 8: The ram and the goat   36

Daniel 9: Pleading for the nation   50

Daniel 10: The man in linen   64

Daniel 11: Battle of the kings   75

Daniel 12: The end will come   91

Appendix 1: The Son of Man and the   104
holy people of the Most High

Appendix 2: The 'seventy sevens'   107

Appendix 3: The Maccabees   109

Preface

This book is mainly built on sermons I preached at Kensington Baptist Church in Bristol – a continuous series on the second half of Daniel. The book is also informed by close and extended study of the book of Revelation, with which Daniel (most obviously in chapter 7) shares such close connections. I have described Revelation as a survival manual for Christians, and in its Old Testament context, that is really what Daniel is too.

Those sermons on Daniel 7-12 were also my final preaching efforts at Kensington, where I served on the staff for sixteen years. This book is dedicated, with my love, to God's people there.

Introduction

Daniel is a book that Christians both love and fear! They love the tales of brave Daniel and his friends defying pagan kings like Nebuchadnezzar and Darius, heroically facing the terrors of the fiery furnace and the lions' den. But the love runs out halfway through the book. From chapter 7 onwards, Daniel becomes a fearsome compendium of beasts and battles. We might dip our toes into chapter 7 itself, because after all it mentions the Son of Man, and we know that has something to do with Jesus. But beyond that, rarely a step is taken. One unfortunate result is that the second half of Daniel, like much of Revelation, becomes a playground for crazy theories about the history of the world. At their worst, these theories claim to tell us how and when the world will end.

What many evangelical readers may not realise is that Daniel is troublesome for another reason too. According to many scholars, the book is not what it seems. Parts of it at least date from much later than it seems to claim and have nothing to do with the historical Daniel at all. This is another reason why pastors and preachers (who are aware of this issue even if their congregations are not) may hesitate to tackle the second half of the book.

The point of the book I am writing is to explain what the second half of Daniel is *about*, what it is *for* (just as important), and why it is important for *us*, especially those of us who live in the post-Christian Western world in the early 21st century. In order to do that, there is some business we need to do before we get into the text. So in this introductory chapter, we will look at the historical background to Daniel so that we are clear how it fits into the Old Testament of the Bible; then we will tackle the question of what Daniel is doing in the Bible – what is it for; and then we will ask who wrote it and when. I am not going into lots of technical details – for that you can consult the many commentaries that are available, some of which I will recommend later on.

We then need one more preparatory chapter to overview the first half of the book. That is important, not just to take the story up to our jumping-off point, but also because there are contrasts between the two halves of Daniel, and we need to see them both. Then we will get into a chapter-by-chapter study of Daniel 7 to 12.

Historical background

We are familiar with the fact that the books in the Old Testament are not arranged in chronological order. The arrangement gets more confusing around the time of the Exile of the Jews to Babylon, where Daniel sits. Here is how Daniel fits in to the big picture. After the united and mainly positive reigns of David and Solomon, the kingdom of Israel splits in two. The northern half retains the name of Israel while the southern half is named for Judah, by far the larger of the two tribes it contains.

A succession of kings follows in each of the two kingdoms. In the north, they are all either bad or very bad. In the south, there are some good kings interspersed with some ungodly ones. The local superpower now is Assyria. The northern kingdom (Israel) falls under its power and is obliterated. Its people are exiled and disappear from the biblical record. Judah narrowly escapes the same fate, but within a century and a half Judah, too, falls and is exiled. By this time, Assyria's power has been destroyed and Babylon is the great world empire (strictly it should be called the 'Neo-Babylonian empire', but we won't worry about that here). So it is Babylon that takes Daniel and his companions into exile, as Daniel 1 explains.

About sixty years after Daniel is deported, Babylon itself is overthrown by the rising power of Persia (or Medo-Persia – it's really a joint empire of the Medes and

2

Useful dates

612	Fall of Nineveh and end of the Assyrian empire
605	Battle of Carchemish. Nebuchadnezzar defeats Egypt and then deports Daniel and others
597	Jerusalem taken by Nebuchadnezzar, who exiles many Jews but does not yet destroy the city
586	Fall and destruction of Jerusalem
556-539	Reign of Nabonidus, with Belshazzar acting as his regent in Jerusalem
539	Fall of Babylon to the Medes and Persians
550-530	Reign of Cyrus the Great (including Babylon from 539)
486-465	Reign of Xerxes (Ahasuerus) – Esther
465-424	Reign of Artaxerxes I – Nehemiah
334-331	Campaigns of Alexander the Great against Persian empire: 331 Defeat of Darius III and fall of Persian empire
323	Alexander's empire splits into four kingdoms after his death
198	The Seleucid kingdom (Syria) under Antiochus III 'The Great' takes Palestine from the Ptolemaic kingdom (Egypt)
175-164	Reign of Antiochus IV 'Epiphanes': 168 Antiochus expelled from Egypt by Romans 167 Pagan altar set up in Jerusalem Temple 164 Temple rededicated

Persians). Daniel is still there at the start of Persian rule, and he does not return to Jerusalem when Cyrus permits the exiles to do so. The biblical books of Ezra, Nehemiah and Esther are all set in the Persian empire.

But of course, the Persian empire is no more permanent than its predecessors, and after about two centuries it is overwhelmed by the energetic military genius Alexander the Great. Alexander, the son of Philip of Macedon (Macedonia, in northern Greece) conquers a vast swathe of territory that reaches to the borders of India, but dies within a few years. His empire does not survive. Almost at once it is divided into four, each ruled by one of his generals. The two that are significant for the book of Daniel are the Seleucid kingdom, based in Syria; and the Ptolemaic kingdom, based in Egypt. These two are constantly at war over the centuries that follow, until Rome conquers the whole region.

What is Daniel for?

Once we get into the text, we will mainly be asking, What is Daniel *about*? But it's worth asking at the outset, What is it *for*? Daniel has its own unique contribution to make, and it has a different feel from any other Old Testament book; but we should remember that its essential world view is the same as the rest of the Old Testament, and indeed the New as well. It is God who controls history and has made himself known to a special people that he has called out for himself. He has chosen them by grace, shown them his love, given them his Law, provided a land for them to live in, and requires their obedience as their response to all this. In that sense, Daniel is very much part of the biblical mainstream.

To identify Daniel's special contribution, we need to understand a little about the experience of Exile. For many centuries, the people of Israel and Judah had been in charge of their own affairs. At Sinai, a thousand years before this, God gave them the Law and constituted them as a nation that is best described as a theocracy – rule by God himself, through his Law. The entire nation was understood to be the people of God. At the heart of the nation was the Tabernacle, which was then replaced by Solomon's Temple. This was the place where God dwelt among his people and where the sacrifices that made atonement for sin were offered. The sacrificial system was based on the activities of the High Priest who entered the Most Holy Place annually on the Day of Atonement. There had been plenty of corruption in this system, but it was there and the people depended on it.

But now, all that had changed. The nation had lost its political independence and was ruled by a pagan empire, but it was worse than that. The Temple had been destroyed. Sacrifices were no longer being offered. The exiles were unable in any case to make the required pilgrimages up to the holy city. Instead, they must learn to live as a minority community in an alien and hostile culture. How were they to do this? Answering that question is the purpose of the book of Daniel, which spans the entire period of the Exile. It does so in two ways. In the first half, it shows us Daniel and his friends living out their daily lives as faithful believers in the service of the pagan kings. Most of the Jewish exiles will not have lived so close to the centre of power, so in that sense the experience of Daniel, Shadrach, Meshach and Abednego is not typical. But that just made the challenges for them even sharper. So here we see *how the exiles need to live.*

In the second half of the book, which we will focus on, we are shown God's sovereignty over history and the fate of his people. This is revealed through vivid visions and angelic messages. It is the truth that will sustain them through the very darkest times, such as the dreadful persecution that a later generation will face under Antiochus Epiphanes. This is *what the exiles need to know.*

There are overlaps of theme between the two main sections of the book, certainly. God's sovereignty is powerfully displayed in the first half too, especially in chapters 2 and 5. As we shall see, chapters 2 and 7 have a great deal in common. The distinction between the two halves is also blurred by the fact that the book was originally written in two different languages: Aramaic in

5

chapters 2 to 7 and Hebrew in the rest[1]. There are various theories about this unusual feature of Daniel (otherwise only Ezra is partly written in Aramaic: the rest of the Old Testament is entirely in Hebrew). It's hard to find a good explanation for it. Some suggest it was intended that the Aramaic section should be circulated separately, because this section would be of interest to the world at large and not just to the Jews. That makes some sense. But in that case, why does the actual transition to Aramaic occur half way through verse 4 of chapter 2, rather than at the start of the chapter?

We return to the main point. This is why Daniel is such an important book for us today. We do not live in a theocracy, or even – in the UK at least – in a society that could possibly be described as Christian. We too need to learn to live as exiles, to live faithfully in an alien land like Daniel and his friends. The special contribution of the second half of the book is to show us what it means that God is fully in charge, and that as his people we are therefore utterly safe and totally secure.

Who wrote Daniel – and when?

It turns out that the key question is not who wrote it, but when was it written? On the face of it, the answer is clear enough. Chapters 7 to 12 are written in the first person ('I, Daniel'), either directly or in the form of very long quotes from Daniel which account for almost the whole text. Chapters 1 to 6 are written in the third person about Daniel and his friends, but the obvious assumption would be that Daniel wrote or assembled all the material. So it seems plain that Daniel wrote the book, which places it during his

---

[1] Aramaic is similar to Hebrew and written with the same script. It was the official language of the Persian empire and was therefore a more international language than Hebrew.

lifetime – the sixth century BC. That is the traditional view. However, most scholars take a different line and believe it was written much later. There are various reasons for this, including arguments about the development of language and the use of certain 'loan words' from other languages in the text of Daniel. But by far the major argument for the modern view comes from the prophecies (or apparent prophecies) in the second half of the book. This will become clearer when we look at the text, but we will set the arguments out now. We start with the way the author sees human history playing out.

The second half of Daniel (and chapter 2 as well) lays out future history in terms of a succession of four kingdoms or empires. On the traditional view, these have been understood as Babylon, Persia (or Medo-Persia), Greece and Rome. The consensus of recent scholars, however, is to read the scheme as Babylon, Media, Persia and Greece. We won't be able to go into all the arguments about who is right on that, though we will get back to this in chapter 7. The point for now is that the author of Daniel seems to believe the world will end (that is, God will bring in his final judgement) in the days of the final kingdom – Greece. Obviously, we know that didn't actually happen.

The modern view holds that Daniel was written – or at least, heavily edited – in the time of the Greek empire, more specifically in the days of King Antiochus IV Epiphanes, who ruled over one of the fragments of Alexander the Great's empire in the middle of the second century BC. The author (they say) believed that the crisis caused by Antiochus' persecution of the Jews was going to bring about the end of the age. The purpose of the book is to encourage the embattled Jews to remain faithful to their God, whatever the cost.

Additional note: arguing over the date

Many readers will not concern themselves at all with these arguments about when the book was written. Fair enough – but it does have implications for what we believe about Scripture's authority and its clarity (or 'perspicuity').

From the available evidence, it certainly seems that early Christians were united in believing that the book was written in the sixth century BC and that it's therefore genuine prophecy, as it appears. That was plain enough to them. Yet a prominent modern commentator like John Goldingay can describe the closing verses of chapter 11 as 'providing an imaginary scenario... which is not to be pressed to provide... historical data'. His view of chapter 11 is based on the view that 'it is not in the nature of biblical prophecy to give a literal account of events before they take place'.

With many others, he would also say that such 'quasi-prophecy' is not an exercise in deception, because its original readers would realise that it was intended to provide theologically informed commentary on events that had already happened. I have given my reasons for disagreeing in the main text.

It is chapter 11 – generally agreed to be the most difficult of the book and one of the hardest in the whole Bible to understand – that is the key to this view. Up to a certain point in that chapter (around verse 35), the author has been predicting the story of Antiochus accurately. From verse 40 onwards, at least as it appears, he begins to get the prediction all wrong. The reason is that he hasn't really been predicting it at all, he has simply been telling the story up to his own time, which turns out to be around 164 BC. It is not really prophecy[2]. No wonder the story up to verse 35

---

[2] Some would go so far as to say this means we can date Daniel (or these later chapters of it) very precisely in 165-164 BC. That would make it the only book of the Bible that can be dated to within a year!

matches the history so well. Then when he tries to take the story into the future, because he doesn't really know how things will go, he goes wildly astray.

Now what do we say about that? No biblical books carry a date stamp, of course – but briefly, here is why I am confident that this work comes from the biblical Daniel, as it claims to do; and that it really is true and remarkable prophecy. For a start, that 'history after the event' view makes the whole thing a work of fiction, because the book clearly claims to be prophecy. In particular, chapter 10 and its account of Daniel's frightening encounter with the angel would be completely imaginary, fictional.

Also, that view makes the writer and his contemporaries remarkably naïve. It would be obvious to anyone by this time that the end of Antiochus is not going to be the end of history, because the new power on the block is Rome; and Rome (as we shall see) has already placed a severe limit on Antiochus' pretensions and proved itself more powerful. What is more, within a couple of years of writing it would also be obvious that the writer had been wrong about the end of Antiochus, so the book would never be accepted into the canon of Scripture.

Many of those who take this view do so because they do not believe that predictive prophecy is possible. Therefore, if anything appears to be an accurate prediction, it must have been written after the event. To be fair, however, there are also commentators such as John Goldingay and Ernest Lucas who believe that God is perfectly able to inspire his prophets to predict the future in detail, but think it's extremely that he would work that way.

In this book, I will be assuming the traditional view: that the 'four kingdom scheme' ends with Rome, not Greece; that what presents itself as predictive prophecy really is prophecy; that the stories about Daniel are true stories; and that the book was written by Daniel himself – perhaps with some light editing after his death – in the sixth century BC.

I will make the argument for all these points in the appropriate places. While I respect some of those who argue for a late writing date, I believe that our doctrine of the inspiration of Scripture demands that we take the claims of the book at face value.

There is another point here too. It is true that many of the applications of the book can be made from either of these two points of view, but they turn out to be stronger and more convincing if they are based on a straightforward understanding that the book of Daniel is just what it claims to be.

This is not a technical commentary. However, I have provided some additional notes which you will find in shaded boxes scattered through the text in the appropriate places. These notes provide a bit more explanation of some of the more tricky points of interpretation. Three of the longer notes appear as appendices at the end of the book. Feel free to ignore them if you wish!

I have not made this book dependent on any one Bible translation. I have worked mainly from the New International Version (NIV) and English Standard Version (ESV), as well as the Hebrew text.

Further reading

I hope you will find this book will take you a long way in reading and understanding Daniel 7 to 12, but if you want to study it in depth, you will need more. Here are some recommendations. Joyce Baldwin's *Daniel* in the Tyndale Old Testament Commentary series has stood the test of time. First published in 1978, it's been through various editions and reprintings and I think it's still the best short commentary around. It defends the 'traditional' view of Daniel I have described above.

Also helpful on the conservative side are Bob Fyall's *Daniel: A tale of two cities* and Dale Ralph Davis' *The*

Message of Daniel in the Bible Speaks Today series. I have made a lot of use of Ernest Lucas' somewhat more technical *Daniel* in the Apollos series. He does not hold the traditional view of Daniel but is fair to it, and the commentary is full of useful insights. I'm also grateful for the module on Daniel that Ernest taught at Trinity College, Bristol. Then there is John Goldingay's *Daniel* in the Word series. He holds a similar position to Lucas and the commentary is definitely worth looking at if you want something more technical, though personally I always find the format of the Word series rather irritating!

Overview of Chapters 1 to 6

Before we get into Daniel's visions in chapters 7 to 12, we need to have a good look at the first half of the book. That's what we shall do now, dwelling on chapter 1 which sets the scene. See how Daniel's story begins in verses 1-2. Remember: Babylon has just become the great superpower. Judah, the home of God's people, falls under Babylon's control. King Jehoiakim is forced to submit to Nebuchadnezzar, who will shortly be crowned as king. It is 605 BC, Judah has been reduced to the status of a minor vassal state and Nebuchadnezzar rubs their noses in it by carrying off the sacred contents of the Temple – which will reappear in chapter 5 – and installing them in the house of his own god.

The scene shifts to Babylonia – or, as v.2 actually calls it, Shinar, which is the ancient name and a very pointed one. It takes us back to the Tower of Babel story in Genesis 11 –where humanity shook its collective fist in the face of God. To say 'Shinar' is the Bible's way of telling us that Babylon is not just the historic city, it's a symbol of humanity's persistent rebellion against God. This is what Babylon represents all through Scripture – it's the evil empire *par excellence*.

This city is the home of the Esagil, the temple of the god Marduk, possibly on the very site of the original Tower of Babel. You would enter Babylon down a broad, open street and pass in through one of the eight gates to the city, such as the great Ishtar Gate which Nebuchadnezzar himself will later rebuild, covered in pictures displaying the gods of Babylon[3]. Jerusalem has nothing to compare with this. To

---

[3] The Ishtar Gate has been partially reconstructed in the Pergamon Museum in Berlin (actually the larger half of the gate is too huge for

anyone arriving in this great capital from the fringes of the empire, the message is clear. The power is ours. Resist, and we will crush you.

It is to this awe-inspiring metropolis that Daniel and his three friends are brought, as the following verses tell us. This is a place where no-one knows their Lord; no-one cares about him or his commands. They thought Judah was becoming godless – this place is a million times worse!

Here, then, is the point of contact for us and our own day. We too live in a land where few people know and honour the one true God and where false gods are plentiful and widely followed. True Christian faith is often met with hostility today: people have developed their own morality, and it looks very different from the message of the Bible. It's as if we too have been taken into exile, and like Daniel we need to learn how to live there.

To a large degree, this is exactly what the book of Daniel is about – especially the first half. Daniel and his friends really have three options to choose from. One: they can *assimilate*. They can simply become part of the Babylonian world – which, after all, is exactly why they have been brought here. Their true identity as Jews, members of the people of God, can be quietly forgotten. They can enjoy an easy life and accept all that Babylon has to offer. Two: they can *retreat*. This is a way to retain their identity, to keep themselves pure. They will have to do the daily work they are made to do, but beyond that they will have no interaction with the wider population. As far as possible, they will be safe. Neither of these options will have any spiritual impact on the world around them.

But there is a third option. They can choose to *engage*. They will do their jobs really well so that they are known as

---

the museum to accommodate, so it is kept in storage!). In this form, it dates from around 575 BC, around thirty years after Daniel and his friends arrive in Babylon.

good servants of the state. And meanwhile, they will be involved with the world in a way that challenges what is evil, addresses injustice, affirms what is good and holds on to their identity as the people of God. This third option is difficult, challenging and complex and involves a lot of further choices. Others may shy away from it – but this is exactly what Daniel and his friends decide to do. Chapters 1 to 6 of the book show us what it means in practice. In this way they show us, too, what it will mean to live faithfully for God in exile.

Drawing the line

We continue through chapter 1 as this squad of young Jewish men arrive to be trained up and prepared to serve in Babylon. Verses 5-8 tell us how they begin. It's a fantastic opportunity – a three year degree course in Babylonian humanities, on full support, with a guaranteed job on graduation! It's a demanding course. They will have to learn to write in Babylonian cuneiform; there will be science and maths to study; but there will also be astrology, magic, the reading of omens – morning till night immersion in the pagan world of Babylon, which will try to capture their minds as well as their bodies.

The response of these four young men is to submit. Just as if they have read an advance copy of Romans 13, they submit to the established authority. They even submit to having their names changed. Instead of names that refer to the one, true God, they now bear names based on the gods of Babylon. They throw themselves into their new lives, engaging with the culture even though it is hostile to everything they have known.

However, they do not lose their identity: the time does come when they draw a line in the sand. The issue is what they will eat and drink. Daniel takes the lead, but it is soon clear that the other three are with him. People have debated just why they won't eat the provisions that they are assigned; but what it comes down to is this. In that culture, to eat at someone's table has massive significance, covenant significance. If you share the king's personal provisions, you are the king's man. Refusing his food is therefore a bold, political statement. That is why the friendly official is so reluctant to help (verse 9) – he is worried about being implicated in a palace plot. But Daniel is the Lord's man, not the king's man, so he draws the line.

It is interesting to see how he does this in the rest of chapter 1. He is firm, but also polite. He explores more than one way to avoid showing allegiance to the king. In the end, he finds a way. There is a cost, of course – and not just that they will miss out on the best dinners in the land! They will be marked men now. And almost certainly, there are many from Jerusalem who have not chosen to take this stand. That will make their position harder.

This chapter ends happily. The four men pass the test, graduate top of their class and duly embark on their careers in public service. But sterner tests will follow, as we will now see. Babylon operates in two ways. Daniel would see both of these in action, and so will we. Sometimes it uses enticement, drawing us in, appealing to our desires and our ambitions. That's how we see Babylon in chapter 1. Daniel and his friends are offered the whole world of their day; maybe we will find ourselves in the same position. Then sometimes Babylon abandons its attractive face and turns to threat. Daniel and his friends see that side of Babylon too.

The strategies of Babylon

Babylon always has these two strategies. We see the pattern set out clearly when we meet Babylon again in Revelation 17 and 18. In Revelation 17, Babylon is pictured as the great harlot, who offers us the world in exchange for our souls. Then in Revelation 18, we see her as a city, strong and powerful and oppressive, trading in all kinds of commodities but also in human trafficking. This time, 'Babylon' does not refer to a specific city but to the living, beating heart of godlessness in every age, the evil system of the world. It is what Revelation repeatedly calls 'the great city' that opposes and mimics the heavenly city, the New Jerusalem that is the eternal home of God's people.

The call to 'Come out of her, my people' (Revelation 18:4) is not a call to physical separation from the world, as if we were all to become hermits or monks. It's a call to avoid being entangled with her sins, so that we will not be caught up in her judgement. It is a call to holiness in the midst of a sinful world.

But Babylon will fall. Revelation 18 is a triumphant celebration of the fall of this city that has hated and oppressed the Lord's people. It is precisely the fact that she has persecuted and slaughtered the prophets and saints that ensures her utter destruction, for this is how the chapter concludes. Babylon must have seemed phenomenally powerful to Daniel and company as they were led through those great gates, and as they saw Nebuchadnezzar's temples and other prodigious building projects taking shape around them. Babylon may look very powerful to us too – but Babylon will fall!

Serving and standing

Chapter 2 is set soon afterwards (verse 1). The king has a troubling dream but cannot remember it. He demands that his astrologers tell him both the dream and the meaning, and displays his true character by threatening to kill them if they cannot do this. Daniel and his friends are to be swept up in the mass execution, but Daniel meets the guard commander, is granted his plea for time, prays urgently and has the dream and its meaning revealed to him in a vision that night. Everyone's life is spared and Daniel goes in to the king.

What Nebuchadnezzar has seen in his dream is a giant statue made of a succession of different materials. According to the interpretation Daniel has been given by the Lord, the different parts of the statue represent a sequence of four kingdoms. The first is Nebuchadnezzar himself. The fourth kingdom, however, will see something new. In the dream, the statue is shattered and crushed by a rock that grows to fill the earth. That, declares Daniel, represents an eternal kingdom that God will establish in the days of the final kingdom in the sequence.

Daniel has made it clear that his insight comes from the one true God who knows all things. Nebuchadnezzar responds by honouring Daniel and acclaiming his God. Daniel and his friends are promoted to high office. He has served the king well, saved the lives of others and in all this he has gone out of his way to honour God.

The scheme of four kingdoms or empires which are then superseded by an eternal kingdom is repeated in a different form in chapter 7, which in turn sets the agenda for the second half of the book. The identity of the first kingdom is clear, because verse 38 tells us. There is disagreement over whether the series ends with the Roman empire (the traditional view) or the Greek empire of Alexander and his successors (the modern view). But given that the eternal kingdom that overwhelms all the others must surely be identified with the kingdom of Jesus Christ, we are led to the conclusion that the fourth kingdom must represent the rule of Rome, into which Jesus was born.

In chapter 3 the faithful few, minus Daniel, face the threat of being dropped into a furnace if they will not worship the king's golden statue. It's possible he has taken the idea from the dream of a statue he had in chapter 2. But this is where Babylon turns really nasty. The three young men refuse to comply, and Nebuchadnezzar has the furnace heated up even hotter than usual and orders that Shadrach,

Meshach and Abednego be thrown into it. Their response to him is magnificently calm and remarkably brave (verses 16 to 18). They do not know whether God will deliver them or not, but their stand is the same either way.

And, of course, God does deliver them. A mysterious fourth figure is seen to have joined them walking around unharmed in the fire. His appearance 'like a son of the gods' (not 'the Son of God' as older translations had it) suggests Nebuchadnezzar assumes this figure is an angel. The three young men emerge entirely unscathed and fully vindicated. Once again, Nebuchadnezzar praises their God, declares (in typically bloodthirsty tones) that no-one shall speak against him, and promotes Shadrach, Meshach and Abednego. Babylon has tried to do its arrogant worst, but it has failed.

In chapter 4 we are back in Nebuchadnezzar's dreamland. Most of the chapter is actually written as his own report of a deeply humbling experience. First he has dreamed; once again Daniel has interpreted the dream and shared the interpretation with the king; then the dream is fulfilled. The king in his continuing arrogance loses his kingdom and his sanity and is reduced to living as an animal for a period of time. At the end of that time, he is restored to his former position. This time, his response of honour and praise to God Most High seems more like a genuine conversion.

That concludes the stories of Nebuchadnezzar. The final word on this great monarch is that he has been humbled before the one true God. The Lord has again displayed his sovereign power: Daniel has been on hand to serve faithfully both his king and his God.

We now move on a couple of decades. In chapter 5 we are in the final hours of the Babylonian empire. History tells us that Belshazzar is actually a regent acting for the absent king Nabonidus. Outside, the empire is crumbling under the assault of the Medes and Persians. The banquet he holds is a display of power, but also a show of bravado by a frightened tyrant. He goes one further than Nebuchadnezzar by taking the sacred vessels plundered from the Jerusalem Temple for use in his drunken feast. The writing that appears miraculously on the wall is not illegible, it is incomprehensible. Daniel is brought out, dismisses the offers of wealth and status which will very soon be meaningless anyway, and once more interprets, though not before he has reminded Belshazzar of the cautionary tale of great Nebuchadnezzar and his humbling before God. It is a lesson that Belshazzar knows but has refused to learn. The writing is a message of judgement. Belshazzar's days are numbered, his downfall is imminent and his kingdom is doomed. And so it happens. That very night, Belshazzar dies and the empire falls.

Chapter 6 takes us into the Persian era and the rule of 'Darius the Mede', first mentioned at the end of chapter 5. The identity of Darius has caused a lot of debate, because all the histories tell us clearly that it was Cyrus the Persian who conquered Babylon. For those who doubt the reliability of the book, the appearance of 'Darius' here is evidence of confusion. There were three later Persian kings named Darius (the first of whom appears in Ezra and the last being the one finally defeated by Alexander in 331 BC), so perhaps the author has simply got mixed up.

The best explanation is the simplest: Darius the Mede is another name for Cyrus. We know that Cyrus was about sixty when he conquered Babylon: the end of chapter 5 tells us Darius was sixty-two. We know that Cyrus was related to the Medes through his mother and that he was also known as 'king of the Medes'. The last verse of chapter 6 might seem to require that Darius and Cyrus are different people, but it is quite possible to translate the text as 'the reign of Darius, *that is* the reign of Cyrus the Persian'. It was very common for kings and emperors to be known by more than one name – we know of plenty of examples.

Anyway, there is no need for the appearance of 'Darius' to cast doubt on the reliability of the book of Daniel.

Daniel 6 tells the story of an extreme version of office politics. Daniel's colleagues in the new administration are jealous of him and would like to find grounds to accuse him of misconduct, but his integrity is such that this is impossible. Now in old age, and as he has done throughout his life in exile, Daniel continues to serve faithfully and well. His enemies are forced to be more devious, setting up a scheme whereby people may pray only to the king and then accusing Daniel, who steadfastly continues his usual practice of praying openly to God three times a day. The trap is sprung: Darius is forced to abide by his own decree and reluctantly he enacts the specified penalty of throwing the offender into the lions' den.

Daniel's fate is thus parallel to that of his three friends in chapter 3. And like them, he is delivered by the Lord. Just as the furnace did not burn them, the lions do not touch him. Daniel is saved, the king is relieved and the Lord is praised. Darius, like Nebuchadnezzar before him, issues a decree that all his subjects must honour Daniel's God. Daniel is vindicated and, again, he continues to serve both his king and his God. We might perhaps speculate that this episode spurs Darius (Cyrus) to encourage the Jews (and other subject peoples, history tells us) to return home, probably in the same year in which this story is set.

That story concludes the first half of Daniel. We have seen Daniel and his friends learning to live faithfully for their God in the land of exile, aliens in a strange land. These chapters are full of lessons for us as Christians in the West today: lessons about knowing our identity in Christ, about serving well in our daily work while also serving the Lord; about the value and importance of integrity; and about knowing when to draw the line and refuse the demands of Babylon. We have also seen the sovereignty of God at work in the lives of his people, of pagan kings and of the destiny of nations and empires. And that sets the scene for the second half of the book, which will be our main focus.

Daniel 7: The beasts defeated

Islamic State believed in a worldwide empire. They believed that history was going somewhere – and that history was on their side. On June 29th, 2014, just after they captured the city of Mosul, Islamic State declared the formation of a caliphate. That's a word with powerful echoes of the early days of Islam, when a great empire held sway from the Atlantic to the heart of China, and at one stage came close to overwhelming the whole of Europe as well.

A few days later, the leader of IS, Abu Bakr Al-Baghdadi, made a rare appearance in the ancient Grand Mosque in Mosul. He was now to be known as Caliph Ibrahim, the new Islamic Messiah. At this point, IS was carrying all before it, occupying huge areas of Iraq and Syria and with supporters in many countries in the Muslim majority world, even though most Muslims thought they were crazy. Perhaps their caliphate might even become a reality.

But within three years, the picture looked very different. IS was still capable of terrorist horrors, but its territory had almost all gone and its central power had all but evaporated. Many thousands of IS fighters had been wiped out. They thought they knew where the world was going, but their theory of history proved disastrously misguided.

IS are not the only people to have strong ideas about where the world is going. At the heart of Communism, for example, is the idea of class struggle that will ultimately produce the harmonious, classless society. It never happens. Before the First World War, many people in the West were convinced that the world was becoming a better and better place, entering a golden era of peace. After 1914, that idea no longer made much sense. And yet today, a new generation of atheist thinkers are once more pinning their hopes on human progress. We can fix all the problems. It's going to be all right in the end.

Frankly, none of that seems very convincing. But where do *we* think the world is going? When we see the news today, the world probably seems like a mixture of chaos and outright evil. The stories we like have the good guys winning in the end. But in the real world we know, we can't even be sure who the good guys are – let alone that they're going to win. Is there any reason at all to think that we are heading for anything better? Any hope that good will triumph and evil be overthrown?

The Bible tells us that there is. The Bible tells us that this world is heading for a conclusion, a very clear and positive conclusion where evil is dealt with and God's own people win through. For Christians, this is a very joyful message. And this message is nowhere expressed more clearly than in this great chapter, Daniel 7. Out of these weird and often terrifying images emerges a great message of hope, joy and assurance.

Daniel 7 – the heart of the book

Daniel 7 closes one division of the book and at the same time opens another. The section it concludes covers chapters 2 to 7, which is the section written in the Aramaic language instead of Hebrew. And as you can see in Table 1, this section all fits together in a neat, symmetric pattern[4]. In particular, chapter 7 connects closely with chapter 2 – Nebuchadnezzar's dream of the statue. Both these dreams or visions describe a sequence of four future kingdoms, so naturally we assume they are basically describing the same thing. Of course, there are differences: chapter 2 relates Nebuchadnezzar's dream, interpreted by Daniel, and the

---

[4] The technical word for this kind of arrangement is a *chiasm*.

Table 1: Structure of Chapters 2 to 7

Chapter 2 A dream of four kingdoms and God's kingdom
  Chapter 3 A story of Jews being faithful in the face of death
    Chapter 4 A story about royal pride being humbled
    Chapter 5 A story about royal pride being humbled
  Chapter 6 A story of a Jew being faithful in the face of death
Chapter 7 A vision of four kingdoms and God's kingdom

---

elements of it are fairly simple. In chapter 7 the imagery is complex and vivid, and it comes in a vision to Daniel himself. The features emphasised of the fourth kingdom are different too.

But chapter 7 also introduces the *second* main division of the book – see Table 2. This is the section of Daniel's own visions, written mostly in the first person. There are four of these visions and they all look ahead to the future. All of them seem to fit within the overarching four-kingdoms scheme that is laid out in chapter 7. So this chapter is really the hinge on which the whole book turns: its themes and its scope make it crucial.

Table 2: Structure of Chapters 7 to 12

Chapter 7	A vision of four beasts (kingdoms) and God's kingdom
Chapter 8	A vision of two beasts (the second and third kingdoms) and an evil king
Chapter 9	Daniel's prayer and a vision of the seventy 'weeks'
Chs 10-12	A vision of the 'man in linen' and the account of the great war

---

From the opening lines of each of these visions, we see that we are backtracking by a few years. In chapter 7, we are back at the start of Belshazzar's reign, so in terms of the date, we're somewhere between chapters 4 and 5. Then the other visions run on in chronological order, but they don't really go beyond the date of chapter 6. Daniel 7 has a very important place in wider Scripture too. Jesus' favourite title for himself was *Son of Man*. And the key background to that title, that tells us how to understand what he meant by Son of Man, is right here in Daniel 7. Moreover, the book of Revelation connects to this chapter over and over again, as we shall soon see. In fact, it is foundational for understanding Revelation – so it's a very rich chapter.

One more point before we actually get into the vision. In chapter 7 we enter the writing style or genre called *apocalyptic*. It's a vivid and pictorial style of writing with its own conventions – numbers tend to have symbolic meanings, for instance. The mistake we need to avoid with apocalyptic writing is to treat it as a code to be cracked. The point of the symbols is not to give us a difficult puzzle to solve. No, the point is to illustrate biblical truth – the symbols are signs, not codes! For example, in Daniel 7 the hideous beasts do not simply function as a code for the empires they represent. That would be largely pointless. The empires are described as hideous beasts in order to teach us things about their character and behaviour.

In this chapter especially, the Holy Spirit is giving us not a code to solve, but a theology of history, to give us hope and to teach us how to live.

Overview of the vision

Look at verse 1. We are in 550 BC or thereabouts. This verse is the introduction: from verse 2 onwards, it's Daniel's voice that we hear. *Stage one* of the vision shows us the four beasts – this is verses 2-8. Here is the sea – as it's described as 'the great sea' we should probably think of the Mediterranean – churned into chaos by winds blowing from all the points of the compass. For the Israelites, the sea represented chaos at the best of times, so this is chaos squared! From this turbulent sea emerge four fearsome beasts. They come up in order: one like a lion with the wings of an eagle that are then ripped off; the second like a bear with the remains of its last meal still in its jaws; and the third like a deformed leopard with four heads and four wings.

There's a lot we could say about the detail of these first three beasts; but notice that they are deformed hybrids. They are all based on the fiercest of animals; they are terrifying, and to a Jewish mind in the ancient world, they would feel far more hideous and frightening than they do to us. Remember, for them, wild animals don't inhabit nature series with David Attenborough, for the viewer to enjoy at a safe distance; they are a daily threat to life. And think too of the Jewish Law, with its rules about clean and unclean animals, and about not mixing together things that are unlike. To a godly Jew like Daniel, all that would make the appearance of these beasts disgusting as well as frightening.

But then in verse 7 we get to the fourth beast, and it's worse again. This one can't even be related to any earthly creature. The other three were different from each other; this one is totally different from them all – in its appearance, in its ruthless brutality and in the ten horns on its head. Then verse 8 zeroes in on an eleventh horn which displaces three of the others and has a strangely human appearance. This horn can both see and speak – and there will be more to say about it later!

In verses 9-12 we move to *stage two* of the vision. This is a judgement scene: the judge is an aged but majestic figure; he's named as the Ancient of Days; and he is surrounded by fire – both on his throne, and like a flowing river – and flanked by vast armies of attendants. And judgement is passed on the beasts.

Stage three comes in verses 13-14: the Son of Man. We see again the Ancient of Days, but now into his presence comes a figure who looks like – a man! Just a man, starkly contrasting with the distorted beasts we have just seen. Significantly, he appears with clouds around him, and to him is given an indestructible kingdom that will last for ever, and he is made the focus of the worship of peoples across the earth.

How does Daniel feel as he sees these astonishing sights pass before his eyes? Verse 15 tells us. It's hardly surprising that he feels disturbed! So, verse 16, he finds someone to ask for an explanation – presumably it's an anonymous angel – and in the rest of the chapter, that is what he gets. Of course, this explanation helps us enormously. Although there will still be some details that are difficult, the essential meaning of the vision is made wonderfully clear in vv.17-27. By the time he has received the interpretation, Daniel is shaken to the core by this experience (verse 28). But what about us?

Our world is a brutal place

Look at verse 7. The Bible has no illusions about the appalling reality of evil. This world is fallen; it is full of sin; it stands in rebellion against God. That's what these four beasts show us. We are told in verse 17 that the beasts stand for kings. 'Kings' and 'kingdoms', in fact, are used interchangeably here – the four beasts are not individuals, they are empires. Their horrible appearance is a picture of humanity contorted and twisted out of shape by sin, especially when our rebellious nature takes corporate form as a tyrannical empire.

Now these four beasts do represent specific, historical empires, just as they do in chapter 2. Despite the crazy ideas you can find on the internet and elsewhere, they are empires of the *ancient* world[5]! The first beast stands for Babylon. In the loss of its wings and being given a human mind, there may be an echo of Nebuchadnezzar's humbling in chapter 4. Certainly, lion and eagle are both used by Jeremiah to describe Nebuchadnezzar (Jeremiah 49:19-22). The second beast stands for the empire of the Medes and Persians which will very soon follow. The third beast stands for the Greek empire of Alexander and his successors: the rest of the book will take a close interest in them, as we shall see. The fourth beast stands for the empire of Rome – and yet it's more than Rome.

Notice how often we are told that the fourth beast is different from the others, that it cannot be compared to anything on earth. It seems to be in a class all of its own, as if we are being told that this is something greater than a merely earthly empire. And it is this fourth beast that gives rise to the mysterious 'little horn', verse 8. We need to look more closely at him. The rest of the chapter tells us more – look at verse 11a and then verses 20-26.

It is startling to read that this 'horn' represents someone or something that will attack and overwhelm God's people. So who is this? Some Roman emperor? Some figure in later history? Some end-time antichrist? Or perhaps even all of these? To help us understand this, we need to jump to the end of the Bible. Now we will see why Daniel 7 is foundational for the book of Revelation. Look at Revelation 13:1-8. You can see at once how closely this vision of the Beast of Revelation ties in with Daniel 7. There is just one beast: it sounds very like the fourth beast of Daniel but it features body parts from the first three.

---

[5] There are some strange ideas out there. One scheme that crops up on various websites matches the first beast to Britain (a lion whose eagle's wings were removed to form the USA), the second to Russia (often described as a bear), the third to Germany (which builds 'Leopard' tanks and whose bird's wings represent France) and the fourth to a future one-world government led by the Antichrist.

See what this beast does. It speaks boastfully and it blasphemes God, just like the little horn in Daniel. It makes war against God's people, and it conquers them. And it rules for a period of forty-two months, which corresponds directly with the period in our verse 25 – 'time, times and half a time', that is three and a half *years* or forty-two months. We will meet this same time period in chapter 12. In Revelation, that period symbolises the whole of the current age, the church age, the time we live in now[6]. The visions of Daniel and John in Revelation are clearly describing essentially the same thing – it's just visualised and expressed in slightly different ways.

The beast of Revelation stands for the power of godless tyranny throughout the present age. When Revelation was written, that certainly meant the

Additional note: the little horn

You may be aware, or you may have read in the Introduction, that many people think the fourth kingdom represents Greece, not Rome, and the 'little horn' therefore stands for the great persecutor of the second century BC, Antiochus Epiphanes. In the next chapter, I will explain why I prefer the line I'm setting out here. For now, be assured that as far as the main message of this chapter is concerned, it doesn't matter.

Roman empire that dominated the world of its day. But, like the fourth beast in Daniel, it means much more than Rome. It is *every* earthly power that has raised its head against the living God and persecuted his people. The

---

[6] For more on this and how the period of forty-two months or 1260 days, which runs through the central section of Revelation, represents the church age, see my Revelation commentary, *The Final Word* (second edition, 2017).

fourth beast includes the great empires of Stalin, Hitler and Chairman Mao in the twentieth century. It includes the power of the ayatollahs in Iran, Kim Jong Un in North Korea, Xi Jinping in China, and even our governments here in the West as they begin to move against the Church.

The horns of these beasts are individual powers that express this 'beastliness' down through the ages. The 'little horn' is one of them – perhaps the worst, yes, perhaps an end-time antichrist who is yet to come. Perhaps.

Certainly, those commentators who have looked for a historical reference in the 'ten kings' and 'three kings' of verses 7-8 and 24 have generally found it a frustrating experience: it's more likely that these numbers are symbolic. The point here is not to decode the vision, nor to construct charts of the end times, but to hear the message and to be ready. Our world is a brutal place, and we should not be surprised by the horrors that we will hear of, even when they are directed against our brothers and sisters – or even when they come for us.

We need to understand that evil is real, and that it is very deep-rooted. Revelation 13 tells us who it is that inspires these evil empires. It's the dragon – that is Satan himself. Revelation 12 tells you all about him. These powers that rage against God's people are satanic. The evil goes very deep, and it cannot be fixed. Military power, diplomacy, economic pressure do what they can, but the evil doesn't go away because it comes from the devil stirring up the muck that's in all our hearts. It keeps coming back. That's what this age of the world is like.

And there is no progress. There are still people who believe that this world can move onwards and upwards through scientific advances and the secular miracles of medicine, so that humanity can fix all the problems unaided. The message of Daniel 7 is exactly the opposite. The final beast in line is the worst of the lot. It doesn't get better, it gets worse.

Look again at verse 21. We should pray for the persecuted church. They are our family. They need us to pray. And when persecution comes to us, as it will, we will want them to pray for us, and teach us how to stand! Our world is a brutal place. We should not be surprised. On the other hand, as we see next, we should not be afraid either.

Our God is the sovereign Judge

Look next at verses 9-10. The Ancient of Days, of course, is a picture of God himself. Despite appearances, God really is on the throne. We see him here surrounded by the fire of holy judgement and by vast hosts as he sits to give his verdict. Again we are reminded of Revelation, and the throne-room scene of chapters 4 and 5. What do we learn from this stage of the vision, this judgement scene, in verses 9-12?

We see that God judges with justice – verses 11-12. The fourth beast and the boastful horn are thrown into the fire, their evil deeds punished and paid for. Now verse 12 is probably the most mysterious in the chapter. Beast-empires one to three are tolerated for a bit longer. This could refer to the way that nations endure longer than their empires – like Persia or Greece of old, or even like Britain in modern times. These nations may endure for centuries after their empires have disintegrated. What the verse definitely means is that God does not deal with all these empires in exactly the same way. He judges on a case by case basis, justly. And – verse 10 – he judges according to the evidence. That's what the 'books' that are now opened refer to.

We see that God judges in his own time. Why does God permit these earthly tyrants so much time to strut on the stage? Why doesn't he judge them much more quickly? We don't know. Part of the reason we do know is that he wants to give people time to repent. But God moves in his own way and in his own time.

Meanwhile, God is not passive in the world. Look back at verses 2-6. Beast one – a human mind *was given* to it. Beast two – *it was told* what to do. Beast three – *it was given* authority. That giving and telling comes from the throne of God. Ultimately, above and beyond what even Satan can do, it is God who puts these rulers in place, God who controls and limits what they can do. It's a message the Bible gives us over and over again. Our God is magnificently sovereign. He is not answerable to us or to anyone else for what he does – he is almighty and all-sovereign, ruling majestically over all.

What does this mean for us? It means there will be judgement for all. It is empires in this chapter, and some arrogant individuals in particular, but one day there will be judgement for *all*. Again we turn forward, this time to Revelation 20:11-15. Again you can hear the echoes of Daniel 7 in this scene of ultimate judgement. There is a throne and One seated there; there are books; there is fire. These are fearful words.

Our rebellion against the living God can endure only so long. One day it will end when we stand before his judgement throne. We are all in this picture. We will not escape it. It's vital that we make our peace with God before that day, so that our names too will be found in the book of life.

Our Christ is the eternal King

Look now at verses 13-14 and then at verse 18. We have seen the hideous, ravening beasts; we have seen the enthroned Judge in his majesty, flanked by angelic hosts – and now, completely unexpectedly, we see a human figure. That is what 'son of man' means. Literally, it simply means 'a member of the human race'. But whatever is someone resembling an ordinary man doing in the middle of such a vision, showing up in heaven and ushered into the presence of God?

What really takes this into a new dimension is that this figure 'comes with the clouds'. In the Old Testament, the one who 'comes with the clouds' is always the Lord, Yahweh in his glorious majesty. This human figure has to be divine! Consider the kingdom and the authority that is given to him (verse 14). This is a kingdom that is worldwide and eternal. And according to verses 18 and 27, the eternal kingdom the Son of Man receives is also the same eternal kingdom that God's holy people receive. That means this Son of Man is our representative – if we are his people, then his kingdom is our kingdom too. People of all nations and people of every language, gathered as the gospel goes out throughout the world. And in some sense, not explained in Daniel, we as God's holy people get to reign with him[7].

We know who this figure is. All of this beautifully describes the Lord Jesus Christ. He, the Son of God, is seen here in his humanity, incarnate as the Son of Man. He is indeed the perfect and truly representative man, the one human being in whom God's image has never been marred, never been broken, the one who never lost what Adam lost for us. He is all that our race was meant to be and failed to be.

When he was on earth, Jesus Christ identified himself directly with this vision. As Jesus faced trial, that night before they killed him, he referred to it directly (Mark 14:61-62). He stood before the religious authorities and confidently claimed all this majesty, this glory, this authority for himself. They will see it – one day they will see it. Revelation tells us that, too (Revelation 1:7). The

---

[7] There is more to say about the relationship between the 'Son of Man' and 'the holy people of the Most High'. You can find this in Appendix 1.

one who was himself oppressed and killed by the fourth beast-kingdom inherits by that death a kingdom of his own: not a beastly kingdom, but a perfect, human one that will stand for eternity.

Questions to discuss or think about

1. The Son of Man is Jesus Christ, the eternal King, who came to bring us peace with God through his death. Do you genuinely believe in him? Are you confident in him, as our eternal King?

2. Daniel 7 is very realistic about the brutal presence of evil in the world. How does this chapter help us to face it – on a worldwide or national level, and personally too?

3. This chapter shows us that history is moving towards a final conclusion and promises that Christ and his people will rule an eternal kingdom. How does that encourage us here and now?

4. Look at the way the vision in Revelation continues (Revelation 13:10b). How will this chapter help you to be patient and endure faithfully?

Daniel 8: The ram and the goat

What do you think of this as a life motto: 'Prepare for the worst – hope for the best'? We could apply it to *national* life. As I write, the Brexit negotiations are in full swing. We should prepare for the worst – no deal with the European Union; but hope for the best – that we will keep all the advantages of being in the EU and have all the freedom of being out of it! This outlook is also the reason why nations have armed forces. We have an army, navy and air force so that we are prepared for the worst – war. But we hope for the best: that those troops will never actually have to fight, because there won't be a war.

We often apply this motto in our personal lives too. At school or university, you probably prepare for the worst – maybe it's going to be a disaster, so I'd better have a Plan B! But you hope for the best – the top grades. And this is also the reason we take out insurance policies. I hope my house won't burn down – but it might, and I want to prepare for the worst, so I have house insurance.

But how does this motto work as an approach to the Christian life? Is this how we should think? Let me propose a slight amendment. 'Prepare for the worst – *trust* for the best.' That is how the Bible teaches us to approach our lives. The worst may come: life may be full of bad experiences. In a fallen world, there is always going to be trouble, and it will end with death. And yet, because we belong to the Lord, we can trust that the best is definitely going to come in its due time.

The vision of Daniel 8 shows that there were terrible troubles ahead for God's people; but glimpsed behind those troubles, like the sunshine gleaming round the edges of a great dark cloud, is the prospect of the best.

Remember the outline of the second half of Daniel, which we looked at in the previous chapter. Daniel 7 gives us the big picture of the four great empires or kingdoms that were coming – Babylon, Medo-Persia, Greece, and Rome. That fourth kingdom, we saw, also hints at something greater and more terrible than the empire of Rome itself.

Here in Daniel 8, the focus narrows as we zoom in on the second and third of those four kingdoms – especially number three – and the events that will take place nearly 400 years after Daniel's vision. The kingdoms are now portrayed by different creatures, considerably more normal-looking than the monsters of chapter 7. Like chapter 7, this is a symbolic vision, whereas the visions in chapters 9 to 12 will be based on messages directly conveyed by angels.

As we look at these visions, we need always to bear this in mind: the point of all this is not to give Daniel, or us, some interesting information about the future. No – it's to teach us great truths about God, and to encourage us and prepare us to stand firm in the trials we face today. That's what this is all about. So with that in mind, let's dive into the vision of Daniel 8.

Overview of the vision

We are told at the start (verses 1-2) that it's the third year of Belshazzar's reign – two years after the vision of chapter 7. Belshazzar, remember, is the last king of the Babylonian empire who features in chapter 5, the story of the writing on the wall. In the vision, Daniel is in a city called Susa, on the Ulai canal. That's not especially important for us here, but Susa will become a great centre of the Persian empire, and in fact it's where we meet Nehemiah working at the start of *his* book.

Then in verses 3-26, Daniel tells us about the vision:

first in verses 3-14 what he sees, and then in verses 15-26 the interpretation that he's given. You see in verse 17 that Daniel is addressed as 'Son of Man': don't be confused by that expression – it doesn't mean Daniel is Jesus! This is the ordinary use of 'Son of Man' which simply means a human being, a mortal man. The angel Gabriel, who speaks those words as he brings the interpretation (from verse 16 onwards), is named only here in Daniel 8 and 9 and then in Luke 1 where he tells Mary she is going to give birth to Jesus, the Saviour of his people. In fact Daniel is the only book of the Old Testament where angels are named at all. An angel, such as Gabriel, is simply a messenger of God.

So we can look at vision and interpretation in parallel. First in verses 3-4, Daniel sees a *ram*: it has two long horns, it charges about and it reigns supreme. What does it represent? No need to wonder – see verse 20: it's the empire of the Medes and the Persians. A joint empire, hence *two* horns, with the Persians representing the later but longer horn, being the more powerful element of the empire. That's quite clear.

Next, verses 5-8, appears the *goat*. The goat gets a lot more air time because he's the focus of the vision. The goat has a single horn and he comes flying in from the west, a picture of energy and high speed. He crashes into the ram and smashes its horns, knocks it to the ground, tramples it into the dirt. What's that about? Quite simple again, verses 21-22 – this is the empire of Greece, and the horn stands for its king, whom we know from history is Alexander the Great.

The description is very true to Alexander's remarkable career. In the space of three short years, he appears out of the west, wins a series of stunning victories over Darius III of Persia and becomes ruler of an empire stretching eventually from Greece right across to India. And all this in his early twenties! But at the height of his power, this powerful horn is broken off (verse 8). Alexander dies at the

Additional note: the little horns

You remember that we met another 'little horn' in chapter 7. It emerged among the ten horns on the head of the fourth beast, which represents the fourth and final empire in the series. That little horn persecuted God's people, defeated them and ultimately was judged by the Lord. And here in chapter 8 there is another little horn.

In the view of many people, the little horns of chapter 7 and chapter 8 represent the same person. The horn in chapter 8 is definitely Antiochus – everyone agrees on that. So that would mean that the one in chapter 7 must represent him too. That in turn would mean that the fourth and final kingdom in the series has to be Greece (Alexander and his successors), instead of Rome. Now in one sense this doesn't really matter. But we do want to understand God's Word correctly. Here's why I think these two horns represent different things.

1. The idea of horns as symbols for kings may sound weird to us, but actually it's fairly common in the Bible. Horns often stand for strength or for a king (as in Psalms 18:2, 75:10, 89:17,24, 92:10 etc). There are lots of different horns even in these two chapters. So two little horns need not necessarily stand for the same thing.

2. The emphasis in chapter 7 is that the little horn is destroyed and then God's people inherit an eternal kingdom. There's nothing about this eternal kingdom in chapter 8. There are several other detailed differences too.

3. Chapter 7 speaks mostly in *symbolic* terms about the little horn, in a way which could suggest he is more than merely one specific character from history. Chapter 8 speaks in very specific *historical* terms and is clearly talking about one individual. For these reasons, I think the two 'little horns' are talking about different things. But it doesn't affect the thrust of the message very much.

age of 32, in 323 BC.

What happens next? As we read here in the imagery of

verses 8-14 and the explanation in verses 23-25, Alexander's great empire immediately falls apart and is split between his four generals, known as the *diadochi*, each of whom take over a piece of his territory. Those are the four horns that replace the one. Out of one of them, verse 9, appears a small horn that grows big and envelops what is described here as 'the Beautiful Land', meaning Israel, the home of God's people. This small horn is going to give them a lot of problems.

Historically, we know that this final horn represents an evil character called Antiochus Epiphanes who is one of the line of kings in one fragment of Alexander's empire. Antiochus IV, as he is officially known, reigns from 175 BC; and he becomes the worst persecutor that the Jews have ever known. We shall meet him again in chapter 11, where we zoom in further to see even closer detail on the events portrayed here.

One more point before we move on. Gabriel tells Daniel that this vision relates to 'the end' (verse 17 and again in verse 19). We should not jump to the conclusion that this means 'the end of the world'. The context tells us that it's about God bringing an end to the rebellion, judging the small horn of verse 9[8].

Now we move on to the meaning of the vision for us.

Prepare for the worst: bad stuff happens to God's people

Look again at verses 9-14 and 23-25, which concern the activity of the small horn, known to history as Antiochus Epiphanes. You see how the vision majors on this man's actions, while the interpretation says more about his

---

[8] And we definitely should not suppose, as some commentators do, that the writer of Daniel mistakenly thought that God's judgement on this one individual would represent the end of the world.

character.

Now put yourself in Daniel's position. This man has been in exile from his homeland for over fifty years. He's grown up and grown old here. And his homeland is not just anywhere: it's Israel, it's Jerusalem, the one place on earth where God has made his home, established his dwelling among his people in the Temple. That has now gone. About eighteen years after Daniel himself was deported, the Temple was destroyed and the land is now enemy-

---

Additional note: verses 10 and 12

Reaching for the heavenly host, and throwing some of the stars down to earth, probably refers to the little horn's sheer arrogance – he is claiming equality with God. Through his actions, this is roughly what the historical Antiochus did. But throwing stars down may also refer to his deposing other monarchs, such as the rightful heir to the throne, Demetrius.

Verses 11-12 are difficult and puzzling, partly because of serious translation problems. Whose rebellion (or transgression, ESV) is in view? The best option may be to see the transgression of God's own people as the cause of Antiochus gaining the power over them that he does.

---

occupied. Daniel and the other faithful exiles are longing for the day when they can return home and rebuild – as we will see in chapter 9.

But what is he shown in this vision? Some of these verses are a little obscure and verse 12 in particular is almost untranslatable – we're not sure what this 'rebellion' refers to, whether it's about the sin of God's people or the sin of the invaders – but the basic outline of what's coming is clear. It's this: that once again, the Temple will be occupied and the sacrifices will be halted; and that once again there will be a fierce and arrogant invader sweeping through their homeland. In fact, this is going to be far *worse* than before, because this king will deliberately target God's people the Jews and their worship.

You see, when *Babylon* invaded, when Nebuchadnezzar came through, Jerusalem and the land around it weren't really anything special to them. It was just one more little territory that needed to be put in its place. But this character is different. With this man, it's personal. History tells us what happens. Antiochus enters the Temple, sacrifices pigs on the sacred altar, does all he can to stamp out the practices of the Jewish religion, sweeps away all that is most precious and meaningful for God's people. He directly opposes 'the Prince of princes', God himself. This had never happened before – and it would never happen again, not like this.

It's very unusual for such detailed predictions to be given in Scripture. Prophecy doesn't usually work this way[9]. There must be a very good reason for it here. And there is: it's the threat to the Temple. The Lord is telling Daniel, You can't hang all your hopes on the restoration of the Temple, because there is an even worse devastation to come. Daniel is not told how far off these events will be, though he is told they lie in 'the distant future' (verse 26). As it turned out, they would take place nearly 400 years in his future. But he does know that really bad stuff will keep happening to God's people.

If you know your Bible, you'll be well aware that this is not an isolated message. Think for example of Habakkuk, and of many of the psalms. Think of the earlier chapters of Daniel, too. The Bible warns us, time after time, that God's people have to suffer. Antiochus is an especially terrible example, but it's the repeating pattern of history. Tyrants rise, evil ideologies like fascism and communism spring up.

---

[9]This is why some people think this is not actually prophecy, but 'quasi-prophecy' written after the event – see the Introduction for my discussion of that issue. We will return to this in chapter 11.

Recently, the world has commemorated the hundredth anniversary of the Russian Revolution (1917), which led to the deaths of tens of millions of people and the destruction of many thousands of churches.

'Truth was thrown to the ground', says verse 12. How contemporary that sounds – it's fake news! In the Soviet Union, the Communist Party's official newspaper was called *Pravda*. Pravda means *truth*. What an ironic name for a paper that specialised in lying to the people! That's a classic example of the propaganda machine of tyrants like Antiochus. And the Church is always in the firing line. God's people in the Old Testament faced such tyrants; and God's people in New Testament days down to our own times face them too.

It is the normal state of affairs that the world hates God's people. It's what God's Word tells us, and it's what we see in history. The Lord will sometimes allow shockingly successful assaults on his people. Like Antiochus, they will prosper in everything they do. Think of North Africa. Today, we know it as solid Muslim territory: the church of Jesus Christ barely exists there. But in the early centuries after Christ, North Africa was one of the great heartlands of Christianity. Then all that was swept away by the invasion of Islam. Only now, about thirteen hundred years later, is the Church beginning significantly to grow again there.

We think of France as spiritually dead. Yet after the Reformation, France was ablaze with spiritual life – until, a century later, Louis XIV crushed the Protestant Church and martyred or drove out many thousands of believers. The land has never recovered. We should not be surprised when the pattern of history repeats itself now – in Iraq and Syria, in Nigeria and China; one day, even here in the West. God's people are never immune from persecution and trouble, until we get to glory. So prepare for the worst.

How does Daniel react to this? Look at verse 27. His reaction is even stronger than it was in chapter 7! This verse does not mean he cannot understand the words he is told, the explanation he is given. He means, as we might put it, 'I couldn't get my head round it.' It is too much to take in. He is horrified by the suffering in prospect for God's people. Remember, these are not people he knows personally, it's not his friends or his family – this is far away in the future. He will never meet the believers who will be crushed by Antiochus. But he *feels* for them!

We must beware of studying these chapters just so that we can say, At least I've got a bit of a handle on these tricky bits of Daniel. We are supposed to feel what Daniel feels. We are supposed to suffer with God's suffering people today: to feel for the ravaged churches in many parts of the world – buildings burnt out, leaders slaughtered, congregations scattered – as if they were us. *Our* buildings, *our* leaders, *our* people – burnt, imprisoned, killed, scattered. When one part of the body suffers, the whole body is in pain.

When we feel for them, we will start to pray for them. And we will understand a little better that we need to be ready too. The trouble that some of us already face for being Christians here in the West should warn us that we are likely to face far worse before much longer. Prepare for the worst!

Trust for the best: we are the beautiful people!

Where, then, is the good news in this chapter? Actually, there is plenty of it. For a start, *superpowers are fragile*. As we see in verse 8, these horns are very strong, but they are also very brittle. Did this strike you when you read it? They have a way of shattering rather easily – and that's a great picture of the way that earthly powers so easily fall. It happened with the Babylonians and again with the Persian empire. In our own times, think of the collapse of the Soviet Union.

God can bring down these arrogant powers in a moment, whenever he chooses. The principle that pride goes before destruction is spelled out in Proverbs 16:18. Did you notice in the description of Antiochus, how both his rise in verse 24 and his fall in verse 25 are said to be not by human power? So whose power was responsible? We know the answer. It's the same for the 'horns' of today – Kim Jong Un; or Donald Trump; or Theresa May; or Jean-Claude Juncker; or whoever is dominating the stage as you read this. God is sovereign. Earthly powers are extremely fragile.

The second piece of good news: *the time is limited.* Look again at verses 13-14. I can assure you that there has

---

Additional note: the Millerites

The prophecy of 2300 days in Daniel 8:14 gave rise to the American sect known as the Millerites. William Miller was an American Baptist preacher who concluded that Christ would return 2300 years after 457 BC, the year when Artaxerxes I decreed the rebuilding of Jerusalem (Ezra 7). The date was eventually pinned down to October 22nd, 1844 – when, of course, nothing happened. Millerite teachings had spread through large parts of the United States and abroad. In England, Millerite papers were published in Bristol and Liverpool.

The movement survived the 'Great Disappointment', splitting into several groups, one of which concluded that the 'cleansing of the sanctuary' referred to in Daniel 8 was in heaven, not on earth. The Seventh-day Adventist Church arose out of this third group.

Various other attempts have been made to predict dates in the modern era based on this verse. We should be warned!

---

been a lot of debate over these 2300 evenings and mornings, which do not correspond to any of the other time periods mentioned in Daniel. It's referring to the times of all the evening and morning sacrifices that will not happen – but does it mean 2300 days or 1150 days, since you need one morning and one evening to make one day? And is it a literal period of time or a symbolic one?

It's impossible to be sure, but here's what I think. I take it to mean 1150 days and I think it's a literal period. That is because it doesn't correspond to any number that has symbolic significance; and because the tone of these verses is about straight history – the passage is speaking of literal sacrifices and a literal sanctuary, literal rebellion and literal reconsecration. That time would then correspond to the period of three years and eight days from when Antiochus desecrates the Temple to the time when the Jews take back control and purify it, with a few weeks extra thrown in because the proper sacrifices are probably suspended for a little longer than that.

That makes good sense of the passage – but even if I am not quite right, and it's not a literal period of days, the main point still stands. The time of suffering is *limited*. We hear the cry in verse 13, How long? It is the question that rings out so often in the Old Testament when God's people are suffering. How long, O Lord? An agonising question, very often; a cry from the depths, a cry you may have uttered yourself, more than once. And here, even the angels are asking how long will the devastation of God's people continue.

The point is, there is always an answer to the question. It's just that we don't usually know that answer. But God does! The Lord *always* knows the answer. The Lord has *fixed* the answer. 'The end' in these verses probably means 'the end of this rebellion'. There is always an end. God limits the time of suffering. That's really good news and a real comfort.

The third piece of good news: *the focus is on us!* These chapters are talking about great empires and powerful kings, conquerors like Alexander the Great, along with the huge territories and millions of people they rule. But time and again, the camera zooms in on the little land of Israel, the city of Jerusalem, the fate of God's people. Compare the extent of one of these great empires, such as the Persians, with the minute size of the territory of Israel after the exiles returned. Yet God's eye is on his own people.

It's the same today. Amid the great events of the world, it's easy for us to feel lost: that God has forgotten about us or that we just don't matter any more. Here in the UK, there are times when it seems that everything that felt familiar and stable is being swept away. The foundations have shifted and we're bewildered by the change. But be sure that the Lord's eye is on us, his people. We are not forgotten.

You may feel so alone and insignificant in your school, hall of residence, or workplace, trying to stand for Christ among hundreds of people who don't know him and have no love for Christians, but his eye is always on you. You are not forgotten. Don't be afraid.

The fourth and last piece of good news: *we are beautiful!* Look at verse 9. The beautiful land was the land of Israel and the people who lived there. Antiochus thought it was detestable and he wanted to crush it; but in God's sight, it is *beautiful*. It's a good translation. And that is us! The beautiful people in God's sight are not catwalk models or the wealthy living on luxury yachts. The beautiful people are us. God sees us as beautiful right now, because his Son, Jesus Christ, has died for us, and we have been credited with his perfect and beautiful life.

That's quite a lot of good news! And it is not blind optimism but solid fact. We can trust God for it. The best news is that there is a future beyond this world and all its troubles. If we belong to the Lord, there is a beautiful homeland waiting for us that will never be invaded, there is perfect worship that will never cease, all because of Jesus Christ.

How do we live as God's people? We prepare for the worst – because in this world, there will always be trouble. And we trust for the best – waiting, expecting, confident for the best.

The Lord Jesus had something to say about all this. In John 16 he is speaking to his disciples, preparing them for his own imminent death and the suffering they will face. The world will hate you, he has just told them. In John 16:1, he tells them why he has warned them so clearly: he wants to keep them from giving up. We too have been warned to prepare for the worst, so that we too will not fall away when the worst comes, but have courage and strength to stand firm. And in the last verse of the same chapter, we find Jesus giving them the wonderful reassurance that they can be confident because he has overcome the world. (John 16:33).

God in Christ has overcome! Christ has died, but Christ has risen! Death is defeated and our salvation is won. Nothing and no-one can take that away from us – no earthly tyrant, no government order, no power of death or Satan. Because of that, we can trust him for the best.

Questions to discuss or think about

1. 'Prepare for the worst – trust for the best'. What do you think of that as a motto for the Christian life?

2. God's people in Daniel's time were liable to pin all their hopes on the restoration of the Temple, rather than on the Lord alone. What secondary sources of hope are we liable to rely on? What are the dangers of doing so?

3. Do you have trouble thinking of yourself as part of a 'beautiful people'? Why might that be?

Daniel 9: Pleading for the nation

Climbing a mountain can be a frustrating experience. It's hard work. You struggle onwards and upwards, focusing on the next objective, the next rise in the ground. The top always seems just out of reach. Most of the time, you can't see very far ahead. Sometimes the mist rolls in and you can't see anything at all. In those moments, you wonder if you're lost, and whether you will ever reach your destination.

But eventually, the moment comes when you attain the summit and every direction is down. The mist rolls away and suddenly, you can *see*. There below you, the landscape unfolds. Stretching away into the distance, range upon range of hills and valleys, disappearing into infinity. It's magnificent, it's glorious, it's beyond all expectations. And you know that all the struggle was worthwhile.

Praying is a bit like mountaineering. Often, it's a struggle. It feels like hard work, and frustrating. Often, we can't see the way ahead. But then there are moments of glorious revelation, when the mist rolls away and we see what we never expected to see. We thought we knew what we were praying for; we thought we knew how God ought to answer. But when he does, it's above and beyond all that we anticipated. That's certainly what it's like for Daniel.

In chapter 9 of his book, Daniel knows what he wants to see. He's experienced the struggles of prayer; he has laboured to reach this point and suddenly – he is *there*. The answer comes. But the answer takes him far, far beyond what he expected: to see more of God's plans, more of his deep wisdom, and more of himself.

Like us, Daniel is concerned about his immediate priorities, and that's what he prays for. And he receives God's assurance. Yes, I will look after those concerns of yours, but I'm going to show you much more – show you that my plans go far beyond what you've ever thought, and that I have everything else in my hands too.

We will follow Daniel on his journey of prayer and see how we can go where he goes. In this chapter, we find his prayer followed by the Lord's response, brought to him once more by Gabriel. A warning: this chapter contains the most difficult section in the book! The last four verses are an absolute minefield, as we will see. But let's get back into Daniel's story, see what transpires, and then see what we can learn for ourselves.

Overview of the chapter

The first three verses introduce us to Daniel's prayer. We're in the first year of Darius, described as the son of Xerxes. Probably this Darius is another name for Cyrus: I have said more about that in the overview of chapters 1 to 6. Cyrus could be described as a Mede because he was related to the Medes as well as the Persians; and Xerxes (Ahasuerus in Hebrew) may well be a royal title rather than a personal name. He certainly isn't the Xerxes we meet in the book of Ezra.

But whatever we say about Darius, verse 1 shows that we are now in the age of the Medo-Persian empire. Babylon has fallen and the Persians are in charge. It's about ten years on from the vision of chapter 8. And we find Daniel in a very good place, because he is studying the Scriptures – specifically, the prophecy of Jeremiah about the Exile. In fact, we can pin down the passages he's looking at: they will be Jeremiah 25:11-12 and 29:10. Jeremiah speaks of seventy years during which the land of Israel will be under the thumb of Babylon; and then will come restoration.

Scholars differ on how we should take those seventy years. Is it a literal number (probably a round number, in this case), or a symbolic one? Certainly from what Jeremiah says and from what Daniel is expecting, the Exile will have a definite conclusion. If the period runs from Daniel's own deportation in 605 BC to Cyrus' decree in 538 BC, which encouraged the exiles to go home, the length of the Exile would work out at sixty-six years, which could easily be rounded to seventy. We'll say more about symbolic numbers later, but in any case, Daniel's prayer shows that he thinks it's time for the Exile to come to an end. However, he doesn't know, and he can't work out, exactly when that is going to happen.

And so he sets himself to pray (verse 3). See how seriously he does this. Now we already know Daniel prays regularly, three times each day (chapter 6). Prayer is built structurally into his life. But this is a special season of prayer. We saw in chapter 8 how deeply Daniel feels the plight of his own people. That comes over again here, not by the kind of direct statement we found at the end of chapters 7 and 8 but simply from the tone and setting of the prayer. He fasts from food to devote himself to prayer. He wears sackcloth and ashes as a visible sign of sorrow and repentance. His prayer is deep, and earnest; and yes, praying like this will be a struggle, tiring and hard. But he prays on.

Verses 4-19 give us the prayer Daniel prays. This is one of the great prayers of the Old Testament. It has a lot in common with the prayers in Ezra and Nehemiah (see Ezra 9:6-15 and Nehemiah 1:5-11 and 9:5-37), where leaders of God's people take it on themselves to plead with him for mercy and grace. The prayer falls into two main sections – first the confession, then the plea.

Confession

The confession comes in verses 4-15. Daniel begins with the nature of God himself, verse 4. We see here that God is *great*, God is *awesome*, God is *loving*, God is *faithful*. We need to know all those things about God if we are to approach him in prayer. Prayer is pointless and God can never answer our prayers, unless he has power and he cares! Daniel gets that clear at the outset. Addressing the Lord in this way is an act of worship.

Then comes the confession of sin, in verses 5-8. The nature of that sin is spelled out throughout the prayer – they have turned from God's commands, they have ignored the prophets he has sent, they have actively rebelled against him. See how Daniel assembles a list of the guilty, from those kings of Judah and Israel who led the people astray, the lesser rulers too, their ancestors and, in fact, everyone who lived in the land, verse 6. It's comprehensive. Before God, the people have not a shred of honour – in the sight of God they are buried in shame. It's a story of dis-grace.

Now of course, we want to say, But Daniel, you're not guilty of any of that! Look how obedient and faithful you have been, even risking your life to serve these pagan kings without compromising your faith in the Lord. Look at your honourable record of serving him! But Daniel knows he is a sinner too. He knows he belongs to this sinful people. And if *he* doesn't come to the Lord to plead for them, who will? Like Ezra in his book, Daniel is innocent of most of the charges he confesses, but he is here to plead for God's mercy on his people.

In verse 9, we find the first gleam of hope, the first ray of light in the darkness. God does show mercy and he does forgive, so perhaps there is a chance. This light will get brighter later on; but first it gets darker again. Daniel goes into detail about the people's disobedience. They really shouldn't be surprised at the disaster that has befallen them, verse 12. The Lord has done exactly what he set out in the Law. Break my covenant, and in the end, this curse of exile will fall on you. So there should be no surprise; they certainly cannot complain that he hasn't done what he said.

The next few verses repeat the theme – disaster, disaster, disaster. What's happened to us is unprecedented, says Daniel. Why? Because Jerusalem is unique! God has allowed *his own house* to be destroyed and abandoned.

Pause here before we move on. We can never have too much of looking at the Lord, and his great and holy character, and seeing our sin in the light of his perfection. Before we ask him for anything, we need to have this clear sight of what the Lord is like and what we are like.

Plea

The plea comes in verses 16-19. Only in verse 16 does Daniel begin to make requests. This verse summarises his plea, and we'll return to it later. See what he asks for in these verses. Turn away your anger; look on the desolated Temple with favour once more; forgive us; take action; see and rescue and restore. Don't delay. Lord, I plead with you to act.

Response

God responds to Daniel's prayer! Gabriel arrives, whom we met in chapter 8. He flies in as Daniel is still praying, verse 21[10]. It's interesting he is described as a 'man' here – all the messengers in these chapters are described as 'men' even though they are clearly angels and able to fly – this is not the evening Easyjet flight from heaven, after all! Calling him a 'man' tells us that his appearance here is basically human, probably for Daniel's benefit. Gabriel arrives and says, I'm here to help you understand, I've come under instruction in response to your prayer; you are

---

[10] Reference to 'the time of the evening sacrifice' does not imply that the sacrifices in Jerusalem has actually resumed at this point. It is how a faithful Jew would be likely to describe that time of the day.

loved and valued by God. Here's what I have to tell you.

This opening shows us that the following passage must be a response to Daniel's prayer for his people and the city. That will help us to understand. However, verses 24-27 are extremely difficult. One prominent commentator[11] on Daniel described the attempts to understand these 'seventy weeks' as a 'dismal swamp' of biblical interpretation! Still, we shall venture in!

The first thing to notice in this passage is the string of footnotes, at least in the NIV, which counts nine footnotes on just four verses, all giving alternative readings. That reflects the difficulty of translating this passage properly. There are points where we can't be certain what the text actually means. Then there's the problem of whether these seventy sevens are a literal or a symbolic period of time.

We could devote many pages roving through the theories and thoughts that people have had about this passage. I'm not going to inflict that on you here. Instead, I will say what I think about these verses and why, and describe one alternative view in Appendix 2.

Almost everyone agrees that these seventy 'sevens' or 'weeks' represent a period of *years*. The timescales involved in doing everything described here demand an extended period anyway. Beyond that, there is disagreement. Most modern commentators think that the events described here culminate in the career of Antiochus Epiphanes, the anti-hero of chapters 8 and 11. He would then be the ruler referred to in verse 26, and the abomination described in verse 27 would refer to his desecration of the Jerusalem Temple. However, this view does not do justice to the language in verse 24 about bringing an end to sin, atonement and eternal righteousness. Moreover, as a matter of plain historical fact, Antiochus did not destroy the city or the sanctuary (verse 26). For these

---

[11] J.A. Montgomery, writing in 1927.

reasons, I think we need to look elsewhere for an explanation.

Look at verse 24 first. Gabriel rattles off a list of six things that will happen by the end of that period. The first three are basically about dealing with sin – a permanent solution to the problem of sin, and an end to it for ever. That must be referring to the ministry of Jesus Christ. His sacrifice for sin provides full atonement and eventually makes possible a new world where sin will no longer exist. Nothing less than that really fits the language Gabriel uses here.

The second three items on Gabriel's list build on that solution for sin. God will provide eternal righteousness through the death of his Son; he will *seal*, that is complete and own everything that the prophets have foreseen; and he will 'anoint the most holy'. The word 'place' isn't in the Hebrew text. So it can refer to the *Temple* being restored – the Most Holy *Place* – and also, as we can see from our standpoint, the Most Holy *One* – the one who declared that he is greater than the Temple (Matthew 12:6) – the anointed *one*, the Lord Jesus Christ.

So Gabriel has made a lightning sketch of God's purposes, fulfilled through the one who is to come. Now he carves out the timescale. What is this 'word' in verse 25? Most people think this is either Cyrus' decree that the exiles could return home, or one of the later decrees about the city and the Temple. But I think, from the use of the expression 'the word going out', it's more likely to mean Jeremiah's prophecy, specifically the one in Jeremiah 29:10-14. It's a *prophetic* word going out from the Lord. That gives us the starting point for the seventy sevens of years.

How are we to understand these time periods? We need to ask what else in the Old Testament went in periods of seven years. Answer: the sabbath cycle of giving rest to the land. It's set out in Leviticus 25. A period of *seven* sevens made up the period of Jubilee. And in the year of Jubilee, slaves were released and they could *go back home*. So it seems very likely that the first seven sevens in Daniel 9 symbolically represent the Exile period, after which the exiles can go back home. And 2 Chronicles 36:21, where the Exile is described, confirms this idea: it talks about the land enjoying its *sabbath rests* during the Exile.

Now in the NIV in verse 25, there is no pause between the first seven sevens and the sixty-two sevens which follow. But that's because the NIV at this point has chosen to follow the Greek translation, rather than the Hebrew. I think the ESV has got it right. The Hebrew of verse 25 then says that '*an* anointed one' will come after the first seven sevens.

Who is this anointed one? That would be Cyrus, who allows the exiles to return home – very soon after Daniel's prayer, as it turns out. We might think that a pagan king like Cyrus could not be described as 'an anointed one', but in Isaiah 45:1, Cyrus himself is described in exactly that way[12]. (So far, by the way, modern commentators might agree with most of this interpretation; but from this point on, they would differ.)

After Cyrus, there are sixty-two sevens followed by the final seven. During the sixty-two sevens, Jerusalem gets rebuilt and restored: streets for people to live in, and defences to protect it. Troubled times they certainly were. Then, at the end of that period, *another* 'anointed one' appears and is put to death. That's the Lord Jesus, the Messiah! Soon after that, destruction comes to the city once more. The ruler in verse 26 refers to the Jewish War and the fall of Jerusalem and the Temple in AD 70 – as Jesus himself clearly foretold. So the ruler is the Roman general

---

[12] However, it is also quite possible that the 'anointed one' in verse 25 is one of the two key Jewish figures involved in the return in Cyrus' time – either Zerubbabel or the High Priest, Joshua.

Titus (or possibly his Emperor, Vespasian).

What about verse 27 and the final week? The account runs straight on into the seventieth week and both verse 26 and verse 27 are describing it. This seventieth week is where we are today. It runs from the ministry of Jesus until he returns and brings in his kingdom of eternal righteousness – the completion of God's purposes as set out in verse 24.

The *abomination* referred to here, again, will refer to the events of the Jewish War, the chaos and sacrilege in the Temple during that war and eventually, the destruction of the whole Temple – which ensured that there could indeed be no more sacrifices and offerings there[13]. Jesus uses precisely this language to describe the tragedies of the Jewish War in Mark 13:14.

I don't claim to be sure of all the details. A couple of points I am sure about, though. One is that these are *symbolic* years, not *literal* years. In that way, one 'seven' can stand for thousands of years. Many people have tried to force these seventy sevens into a literal calendar from the Exile to the time of Christ and beyond. I could give you a long list of the combinations that have been tried. It doesn't work. It's a dead end, or as our friend the commentator said, a dismal swamp.

The other point is that the seventieth seven is not cut off from the first sixty-nine. It can't refer to a separate seven year period off in the distant future. Many Christians have followed that line: they've made verses 26-27 into a precisely timetabled plan of the future end times (see Appendix 2). When you hear people speaking earnestly about 'Daniel's seventieth week', that's what they mean.

---

[13] So this abomination is not the same as the one referred to in Daniel 11:31 and 12:11 (as modern commentators would assert). However, there is certainly a repeating pattern at work in history; and there are certainly parallels between the actions of Antiochus in the second century BC and those of the warring parties in the first century AD.

But this text really gives no support to that idea.

If, then, this chapter is not here to give us a detailed chart of the end times, what is it here for? Answer: simple – it's here to teach us about God and about prayer!

In prayer, we respond to the glory of God's character

Look back at verses 6-19. Verse 16 sums it all up so beautifully. Daniel is pleading with the Lord to turn his anger away. What does Daniel appeal to? Firstly, he appeals to *God's character*. Remember, that's how his prayer begins in verse 4; and he's kept coming back to God's righteousness, and how he keeps his promises, and how he is loving and merciful. As he says in verse 18, I don't ask because of anything good in us, but because of your mercy, Lord.

Prayer springs from knowing God as he really is: incredibly loving and infinitely holy. We look at God in his perfections as we come to him in prayer. Most of all, we today can come with confidence because we know *how* his anger is turned away from his people – it's through Jesus Christ, who took all God's wrath upon himself, atoning for our wickedness (verse 24).

Secondly, Daniel appeals to *God's possession*. Jerusalem is *your* city. We can pray this too – Lord, we are your people. You have taken us for your own. Father, we are your adopted children. You are not some distant, unknowable deity, you are related to us. We belong to you.

And thirdly, Daniel appeals to *God's glory* – his honour, his reputation. The ruins of Jerusalem cry out to the nations around: this people's God has abandoned them. Look what's happened to his Temple! What kind of God is that? Twice in the following verses Daniel talks about 'your name'. Lord, we want your name to be held up high. We want you to be glorified!

Prayer means engaging with God in his majesty, in his

love, in his glory. He invites us in, he wants us to come and respond to him in all that he is. Probably as you have read this chapter, you will be thinking – My prayer life is so poor next to this! And perhaps it is. But this chapter can help us.

Like Daniel, we need to give our prayer life time. We will never have a full and intimate prayer life in three minutes a day. See how Daniel has prepared himself and how he takes time over it. If you want to meet with the Lord in prayer, make the time. Don't say you're too busy. If you have time for your friends, you have time to pray. If you have time for social media, or for that box set, you have time to pray! We always find time for what we most want to do.

Daniel is praying in response to Scripture, and that too is a good pattern for us. Let the Bible lead you into prayer and the presence of God. And then, dwell in his presence. Just be there with him. Look at his character. Contemplate his overflowing love, his monumental justice, his profound wisdom, his towering majesty, his devastating holiness. Stay right there and worship – like Daniel. And use this prayer. You'll need to change a few of the words, but what a great prayer for us to pray.

In prayer, we respond to the wonder of God's purposes

Whatever we may think about verses 24-27 and all their difficulties, one point here is very obvious: *God hears and answers prayer!* It's flagged up very strongly here – Daniel actually gets the answer delivered personally by an angel. (By the way, you might be thinking, I'd rather like to have Gabriel fly in with the answer when I pray! Well, before you decide to swop places with Daniel, bear in mind what would go with the territory – abduction, exile, renaming and a night in the company of hungry lions!) We don't generally get special angelic delivery – but the Lord does answer our prayers all the same!

Do you remember what Paul says in Ephesians 3:20-21 about this? The Lord can do what we ask, and he can do immeasurably more than we ask or can even imagine. Or think of Isaiah 65:24, which exactly describes Daniel's own experience here (verse 23). When we are struggling to pray, when it's a battle to believe, let's keep reminding ourselves of wonderful promises like these. The answer will come: perhaps, as here, the Lord will set his answer in motion as soon as we begin to pray. But sooner or later, he will do it. God hears and answers prayer.

Then, we see that *God's plans are bigger than we think.* See how the Lord answers Daniel's prayer. He shows him that what he's prayed is right and good, and the Lord is concerned about it – the fate of the city, the restoration of Jerusalem. And in the answer, the Lord says yes, there *is* a prophetic promise to restore my city, and yes, it is going to happen soon. But that's only part of the answer. Let me give you a glimpse of the bigger picture, and what will happen later on, and you will see how your concern is just one part of the huge canvas that I am painting on.

You may be praying today for something that is really important to you – and yes, it's a good thing to pray for. Some relationship to be put right, or that job that you need, or for that family member to be saved. And yes, the Lord is concerned about that. But his plans are also bigger than we think. God has a big agenda – bigger than our individual concerns, bigger than the needs of your local church. He is concerned for cities and nations and the whole world. As we pray, let's remember that the Lord's plans are bigger than the small corners that we know about.

And lastly, *God's purposes are completed in Christ.* It's the Lord Jesus who stands at the heart of God's answer to Daniel: his anointed one, who will be put to death as the ultimate sacrifice for sin, to atone for wickedness and bring in everlasting righteousness. Yes, God has a bigger purpose. His grand design in history revolves around his Son, the Lord Jesus Christ. Do you know Jesus Christ? None of this makes any sense or provides any hope if you don't.

For all who belong to him, this is what we need to know supremely about prayer. We pray through the Lord Jesus. Our prayers are about him. Our whole lives revolve around him. And we have a future because of him.

Questions to discuss or think about

1. Think about your own prayer life. How does Daniel's example of beginning with the greatness and character of the Lord challenge and help you?

2. What can you learn from Daniel's approach to prayer, in terms of time and seriousness? How can you transfer his example to your own situation?

3. How can prayer help us to have a clearer perspective on world events and on our own problems?

Daniel 10: The man in linen

The film *The Martian* is one of my favourites of the last few years. In the story, an expedition to Mars has to be abandoned in a hurry and one of the crew is left behind, presumed dead. Only he isn't dead. So astronaut Mark Watney, played by Matt Damon, finds himself alone, many millions of miles from home. How will he survive? There's a lot of ingenious stuff he can do to keep himself alive, but there is nothing he can do to get himself back to Earth.

The crucial first step is that he manages to communicate with home. And then, on Earth, massive resources are mobilised to organise a rescue mission. Watney is just one man, but it seems that no effort is too great, no expense is spared, to reach out and save him. Nations sink their differences and work together. And Watney gets to follow all the news of this titanic effort from his place of exile on Mars. How does Mark Watney feel about everything that's being done to get him home? Surely he must feel valued – wanted – loved!

How do *you* feel when you read Daniel 10? If you think, What in the world is going on here?, I wouldn't blame you! Actually, when we read this passage, we should feel *loved*. What shines from this passage is the love that the Lord has for his people, the lengths that he goes to in order to save and rescue us, the value he places upon us who belong to him, the powers that he puts into action, the resources that he pours out to bring us home.

With chapter 10, we have arrived at the start of Daniel's final vision, which covers chapters 10 to 12. Once again an angelic figure has come to speak with Daniel; once again it's a message about the future; and the bulk of that message will come in chapter 11. Chapter 10 (and the first verse of chapter 11, which should really be included!) is an extended introduction to the message. In fact, it's so extended you might be forgiven for thinking as you read it, Come on, get on with it! But chapter 10 is here for a reason.

Overview of the vision

Look first at verses 1-4. This is the setting for the vision. Verse 1 is an introduction to the entire vision in the third person: from verse 2 to the end of the book, we are back with Daniel as the narrator. The description of the message could refer to its content – the great war, as described in chapter 11 (as the NIV suggests). Alternatively, it could mean 'it was burdensome' (as the ESV suggests) – that it's tough for Daniel to receive this revelation, which it certainly is!

We are a couple of years on from the vision of chapter 9: the year is 537 BC, Cyrus is ruling over the Medo-Persian empire and a year or so before this point, he has issued his great edict that the exiled Jews can return to Jerusalem and rebuild the Temple. Daniel doesn't say that, but we know it from the closing verses of 2 Chronicles and the opening verses of Ezra, which give us the date and the details. The prayer of chapter 9 has been answered!

There's a connection here with the last verse of chapter 1, which says that Daniel remained *there* – i.e. serving the ruling kings – until the first year of King Cyrus. It's now the third year of Cyrus, and probably Daniel is finally living in retirement. He's been in exile for nearly seventy years and is probably in his mid-eighties. That presumably explains why he hasn't gone back to Jerusalem with the other returning exiles – he's simply too old to make the long and arduous journey. It may also explain what he's doing by the River Tigris, away from the centres of empire, such as Babylon on the Euphrates – it's his retirement home!

We are told it is the first month of the year. That's the month that includes Passover, normally a time of great celebration, remembering the great days of the Exodus. But Daniel isn't celebrating, he's mourning, he's on a partial fast, and he's not using 'lotions'. That isn't a reference to aftershave, the point is that anointing with fragrant oil was a sign of rejoicing.

Why is Daniel mourning? Perhaps because he is still seeking more revelation in response to the prayer he prayed in chapter 9. And perhaps because, although some of the exiles have returned to their homeland, he realises that the story doesn't yet have a happy ending. Life is tough back in Jerusalem, and the previous visions have taught him that trouble still lies ahead. But once more, this time of special devotion has prepared him to hear the Lord's message.

Suddenly, the vision breaks in. Verses 5-6 describe the figure who appears. Again it's essentially a human figure, said this time to be dressed in linen with a golden belt. No-one is sure where or what *Uphaz* might be: we can only guess it is intended as a statement of the highest quality[14]. But it's his physical appearance that really catches the eye. Topaz or beryl here probably means the precious stone chrysolite, which is gold-coloured: his face dazzles, his eyes flash fire, his limbs glow like metal and his voice is as loud as a crowd.

Daniel is now left alone. His unnamed companions can't even see this figure, but they feel the terror and make themselves scarce. The scene reminds us of Paul on the Damascus road, where his companions see no-one but are struck speechless (Acts 9:7). Daniel feels his own strength ebb away, the colour drains from his face; as the figure starts to speak, he collapses comatose on the ground (verses

---

[14] Some commentators favour translating the word as something like 'fine' or 'refined'.

7-9).

That is no way to hear a divine revelation: so, verse 10, the figure pulls him part-way off the floor and tells him to listen. Daniel hauls himself to his feet. Yes, he is told, the words of your prayers have been heard and I have been sent with an answer. I've been on my way for three weeks, actually – all the time you've been praying and mourning. I was held up, but I had some help from a powerful person named Michael. So here I am, to present you with this message about the future of your people.

Once again, Daniel seems on the point of collapse (verse 15) and can't utter a word. A touch on his lips, and he's able to express how he feels: anguished, weak and breathless. Another touch, another message to encourage him; and at last he feels strong enough to stand, and ready for the message.

Then, with a little more introduction, the message begins in chapter 11 verse 2: 'Now then, I tell you the truth – kings of Persia – kings of Greece' – and the angel launches into the story of the nation's future that we will look at next. Once again, we will see how our God is sovereign over history – these events which are yet to come are already written down (verse 21).

That's the tale of this chapter, but before we can start applying it to ourselves there are a couple of questions to answer. First, who is this man in linen? It's possible that verse 16 introduces a second speaker, but it's more likely that there is just this one individual dealing with Daniel in this chapter. He is identified in the same way in chapter 12. Commentators don't agree on his identity. Some think it is the angel Gabriel, whom we met in chapters 8 and 9. That's possible: but this figure seems altogether more glorious, more powerful and more terrifying than the description of Gabriel.

Others have thought this is actually God himself, in the person of Jesus Christ, ahead of his incarnation. They point to similarities with the vision of Christ in Revelation 1 and also the visions of Ezekiel. Linen has priestly overtones, which some take to point to Christ. But again, I don't think that can be right. As we will see, this individual has been held back by one angelic power – verse 13 – and he's needed help from another, Michael – verses 13-21. God is not held back by angels, nor does he need help from anyone.

The man in linen is simply a powerful angel. He is anonymous, like nearly all the angels we meet in the Bible. There are certainly different classes and ranks of angels; but we don't get lots of detail about that, because we don't need it. Speaking cautiously, this one seems to be greater than Gabriel, but less exalted than Michael, who is described here as 'one of the chief princes'. Second, then, who is Michael?

In the New Testament, Michael appears twice: once in Jude 9, where he is described as an archangel, or chief angel, and again in Revelation 12:7, where he leads an angelic army against Satan. Here, Michael and company take Satan by the scruff of the neck and show him to the door of heaven.

The name Michael means 'Who is like God?'; and he has the special responsibility of protecting and defending God's people. In fact whenever we meet Michael, he's in a conflict of some kind. This passage reminds us powerfully that angels in particular, and the spirit world in general, are real, awesome and terrifying, and have an impact on our lives.

We shall have more to say about these angels later on. But now: why is it that this passage should make us feel loved?

Loved, because we are highly esteemed

Look at verses 11, 19 and remember the context of this

vision. We know from chapter 6 that Daniel is in the habit of praying regularly; we know that his fasting in chapter 9 accompanied prayer; so we can certainly assume he's been praying through these three weeks of mourning and fasting. Verse 12 implies it even if this chapter doesn't spell it out for us. Daniel is dug deep into his life of prayer. And these verses tell us that his prayers are being answered because he is highly esteemed, held in high regard by the Lord. Daniel 9:23 said exactly the same.

We might feel that that's great for Daniel – the Lord thinks highly of him, so he answers his prayers – but that's not me! But actually – it *is* you, if you belong to him. The Lord says he regards us highly too! Think about it: who else in the Old Testament does God say he takes special delight in? The answer is in Isaiah 42:1. The prophet is speaking of the 'Servant of the Lord' – that's the Lord Jesus. The words are echoed at Jesus' baptism in Mark 1:11, so there can be no doubt. And if God delights so greatly in his Son, the Lord Jesus, then he delights greatly in us as well. And so he will answer our prayers. Once we have put our faith in Jesus, we belong to him, we are united with him, and God looks on us as he looks on his Son. He says to us, *You* are highly esteemed. You are greatly loved. I delight in you.

Perhaps you have never had anyone give you that kind of unconditional approval before. If you belong to Christ, it's yours now: friendship with the Almighty, the awesome love of God. Pause to think about that for a moment: Father God smiles down on you, and he is delighted with what he sees. If you are a Christian, this is you.

Loved, because we are strengthened to stand

Look at verses 8-11 and verses 15-19. See how gently this angel, the Lord's agent, deals with Daniel. Three times he touches him, until he is ready for the message. Notice how this theme of weakness and strength runs through these verses – words for strength appear at least nine times, so we can't possibly miss it. And weak is what we are! We prefer to think of ourselves as strong, in charge of events, running our own lives. But in fact, our lives are incredibly flimsy. The toughest of us is only a heartbeat away from death at any moment. Read Psalm 103:15-16 for the Bible's poetic statement of our frailty.

For all our pride, we are really very weak, as Daniel discovers when he is confronted with something very strong, like an angel. Twice he is told not to be afraid (verses 12 and 19); then he is twice told to be strong (verse 19) – as, gently, the angel gets him on his feet to face reality again.

Remember Jesus' words in Matthew 11:28-30 – words of compassion to people who know they are weak and not up to much, words of gentleness and grace to get us standing on our feet again! The Lord Jesus is a good master. He hasn't called you in order to give you a hard time. He wants to give you rest in him. You can trust him to look after you. What are you afraid of right now? Do you feel weak as you think of it? That's good, because you are. But he is very strong, stronger than anyone on earth and stronger than any of these angels. You can trust that future to him. We should feel loved because like Daniel we are strengthened to stand.

Loved, because we are fought for by angels

Look at verse 13 and then verses 20-11:1. The man in linen, whom we have identified as a powerful angel, says that his mission has been delayed by an extended encounter with the prince of Persia, before he gets a helping hand from the archangel Michael. Clearly, we are dealing with some kind of angelic battle here. The one described as the prince of Persia is not King Cyrus. It's an angelic power, an evil spiritual power, associated somehow with the Persian empire.

Additional note: 'territorial spirits'

Here, just as we did in chapter 9, we find a difficult passage that has been used to support ideas that go beyond what Scripture wants to teach us – this time about the spiritual realm. From this passage and a few others, people have developed the idea of what they call 'territorial spirits'. The idea is that every nation, every area, every city and maybe even every street is in the grip of individual spiritual forces of darkness. These powers are able to prevent the gospel from breaking in there. As Christians, it is our job to engage directly in spiritual warfare against these spirits, so that the evil powers can be broken and the gospel of Christ can reach the people.

Our task begins with identifying and naming those territorial spirits. We are supposed to discern the details of how Satan and his servants are operating in each place, they say. Then we employ specific methods of prayer and spiritual authority to overcome and overthrow those powers in the name of Jesus Christ. It's known as 'strategic level spiritual warfare'. Its best-known proponent was C. Peter Wagner.

What do we say about that? This idea does go beyond what Scripture teaches us about the powers of darkness and what we can know about them. Identifying and naming controlling territorial spirits is not what we find the apostles doing in Acts. It's not what we find Paul teaching the churches in his letters. There is a danger that this kind of talk can appeal to our sinful desire to exercise power, to be in control. At times, it can sound more like magic – the power of naming things, the use of specific methods to exert control over them – rather than biblical Christianity.

In this passage, Daniel is not invited to take part in these great angelic battles himself. He's being told about them to give him insight into the vast resources the Lord deploys for his people. But he himself is in no way taking on 'the prince of Persia'. That's left to the angels.

Meanwhile Michael, the archangel, is specially associated with the Jewish people, wherever they are living – God's people, whether at home or in exile. And the man in linen is a third participant in the conflict. He and Michael together do battle against the prince of Persia. Once they have finished with the Persians, verse 20, the power of Greece will come and the battle will continue.

The passage is not easy to understand, but what we can take away from it is this. The spiritual realm is real and active! We need lots of reminders about that, because we live in a culture that for all its interest in trendy spirituality is still basically materialistic. It denies that spiritual forces are real. But as Christians, we know that they are real. Think of the way Paul talks in Ephesians 2:1-7. Before we were Christians, we were spiritually dead. But now we are alive in Christ, we are seated with him in the heavenly realms – which means that we are now fully part of the spiritual world.

It means that we are now targets for Satan's attacks. It means, too, that the angels are mobilised to protect and defend us. We don't know how that works, but we know that it works. (Judaism, in the inter-testamental period and later, became rather obsessed with angels, but we are not supposed to follow their example!) It means also that we understand that there are evil spiritual powers, demonic powers, at work in the world, which are out to ruin our lives and destroy our spiritual effectiveness. And yes, as we see in Daniel 10, they may be attached to specific places or peoples. Perhaps this is how we can account for particularly extreme outbreaks of evil in certain times and places: the Holocaust, or the Rwandan genocide. There are spiritual realities behind the events of history.

Are we supposed to map where these spirits operate, name them and use a fixed routine to overthrow them one by one – as some Christians would say? No. But do we have a lot to learn about spiritual warfare and using the powerful name of Jesus to defeat the enemy? Yes, we certainly do. It is Satan and his henchmen who keep people blinded to the gospel (2 Corinthians 4:4). As we live the Christian life, as we witness to people, and most especially as we pray, we need to be aware of the spiritual dimension to it all. We are certainly in a struggle against deadly spiritual powers. We need the full armour of God for protection and battle (Ephesians 6:10-20).

But here is the big take-away from this passage. As God's people, we are fought over by mighty angels. These awesome, terrifying beings are fighting over little us. God's agents are fighting for us. Look at the resources that our God has deployed to bring us safely home. I won't tell you how *The Martian* ends. But I can tell you how *our* story ends! God brings each of us, every one of us who have believed and trusted in him, safely home.

So this is the message of Daniel 10. Know that you are loved. The Lord expends immense resources to protect you and care for you. Supremely, God sent his beloved Son to live and die for you. Because of Jesus Christ, we are accepted, welcomed, adopted, esteemed. We are strengthened to stand. We are brought safely home. We are loved for ever.

Questions to discuss or think about

1. Think over what it means that you are so warmly regarded, highly esteemed by God, just as his Son the Lord Jesus is.

2. Where do you need the Lord's strength right now? Do you believe that he has the resources that you need? And that he has the wisdom and compassion to give you what he alone knows that you need?

3. Have you ever thought of yourself as being fought over by angels? What impact does that idea have on you?

Daniel 11: Battle of the kings

Niccolo Machiavelli lived around the year 1500. He was an Italian politician, diplomat and writer who's been called the father of modern political science. Today, the word *machiavellian* describes someone who is devious, cynical, deceitful. That's what Machiavelli is remembered for, because of the ideas that he wrote down in his book *The Prince*.

The Prince is really an instruction manual about how to rule. It will tell you how to take control of a country that doesn't belong to you, which ones are easy to take over, and which ones are more tricky. How it's important to make the people love you, by whatever means necessary. It will also tell you not to worry about loving them in return, though it's good to make them think you do! At times, as a ruling prince, you will need to be cruel and violent. You will need to deceive people: you will definitely need to make them afraid of you.

Machiavelli didn't approve of Christian virtues like modesty, and he thought that believing in God's providence was daft, because it's basically the same as trusting to luck. Christianity, trusting in God, only makes people weak and passive. Religion is useful for keeping the common people in order, but that's the only use a competent prince will have for it.

It makes me wonder if Machiavelli had been reading Daniel 11. Almost every aspect of his political philosophy could be based on what goes on in this chapter! Two of the characters alluded to in this chapter even feature in *The Prince* – that's Cyrus and Alexander the Great. What is certain is that Machiavelli's ideas weren't really new. He was just the first person with the wit to write them down systematically and the audacity to recommend them.

We have to recognise that there are all too many rulers and leaders in our own world who seem to be familiar with the works of Machiavelli. Good and honest government seems to be the exception rather than the rule – although, whatever we think of them in detail, the governments we have in the UK are still far better than most. We can be grateful for that.

Daniel 11 seems repetitive, impenetrable and remote. It is certainly the hardest chapter in the book to interpret. We might well ask, What is this difficult and very odd chapter doing in the Bible, and what could God possibly have to say to us through it? I promise you it's worth putting some work in on this chapter. Compared with Machiavelli, it will give us a much better handle on what's going on in our world and why.

Chapters 10 to 12, remember, give us the last of Daniel's visions. Chapter 10 amounts to an extended introduction to the vision. Now in chapter 11 and the first few verses of chapter 12 we have the message that the angel has come to bring. If you look back to chapter 8, you can see that we are being told about the same period of history. Chapter 7 told us about four kingdoms or empires, stretching off into Daniel's future; and chapter 8 narrowed the focus to look at empires two and three, under the guise of the ram and the goat. First the Persians, that is, then the Greeks; and in particular, for a good chunk of the chapter, the story of an evil king who would arise from one fragment of that third empire, depicted as one of the horns from the head of the goat. Now chapter 11 revisits that same period of time, but with greater detail and without the symbolism of beasts and horns.

Overview of the vision

It's the man in linen who is speaking, this fearsome figure

who has just explained his own part in the battle of the angels. What he explains to Daniel now is the battle of the kings. Verses 2-4 give us the setting, quickly taking us up to the main area of interest. The angel begins at Daniel's own point in time, the start of the Persian empire. He foretells four kings of Persia, starting with Cyrus who is in power now; battles with the new power of Greece; then a new and mighty king whose empire is soon broken into four parts. Historically, that fourth Persian king is probably Xerxes (the fourth king if Cyrus is counted as the first), who launched an invasion of the lands of Greece – not yet a unified country at this point – and was soundly beaten at the battle of Salamis in 480 BC. He is the Xerxes of the book of Esther.

The 'mighty king', whose empire is soon split up, is definitely Alexander the Great – the goat with its single horn from chapter 8. After his death in 323 BC, his empire is split between four of his generals. In the next section, verses 5-20, we meet the *kings of the north* and the *kings of the south*. The angel describes a series of kings along with a gallery of other characters and the battles they fight. It's pretty bewildering stuff and it can be difficult to follow what is going on – but most of it can be matched to what we know of the history of the time.

The northern and southern kingdoms here are two of the four fragments of Alexander's empire. The northern kingdom is based in Syria and the southern in Egypt. Each of these kingdoms is ruled by a respective dynasty – the Seleucids in the north and the Ptolemys in the south: the exact boundaries of the kingdoms vary with the battles that are prophesied in this chapter. I've put more detail in the additional note for those who are interested!

The northern king mentioned towards the end of these verses is known to historians as Antiochus III ('the Great'). Among other adventures, in verse 18 he encounters the rising power of Rome, which inflicts defeats on him in 191

Additional note: the four kingdoms

Daniel 8 and (more directly) Daniel 11 both speak of the four kingdoms that emerged from the one 'kingdom of Greece', which history tells us was the empire of Alexander, son of Philip of Macedon. He died of fever in Babylon, in June 323 BC. The cause of death is likely to have been malaria or typhoid – though in typical style, Machiavelli in *The Prince* suggests he was killed by his own army! Initially, Alexander was succeeded by Philip, his half-brother, who ruled jointly with Alexander's own son who was born after his death and was known as Alexander IV. But it was the generals who were really in charge. They were known as the *diadochi*, or heirs. The nominal rulers never held any real power, and soon the four successor kingdoms became established.

Cassander ruled over Greece and Macedonia, from which the empire had originally sprung. Lysimachus ruled Asia Minor and Thrace. Seleucus took control of northern Syria, Mesopotamia and points east; and Ptolemy held Palestine and Egypt. It is the last two of these kingdoms that concern us in Daniel 11. The Seleucid kings, based in Syria, were all (at least in the period covered by Daniel) called either Seleucus or Antiochus, while kings in the Ptolemaic dynasty always had the name Ptolemy.

Initially, then, Palestine was under the control of the 'kings of the south'. It would be fought over several times during the next two centuries.

and 190 BC – remember the numbers count downwards in years BC! Then he dies, and his successor (Seleucus IV) is left to deal with impossible debts – so, verse 20, he makes an effort to raise extra taxes. But he gets murdered in a conspiracy organised by his prime minister.

All this sets the scene for the main character of this ch, and verses 21-35 are a sketch of his career. Step forward, king of the north, Antiochus IV, whom we have already met in the vision of chapter 8. His introduction isn't very positive – 'a contemptible person', verse 21. He launches a series of successful military operations which culminate in two invasions of the kingdom of the south. The first one, verses 25-28, is pretty successful, though he isn't able to secure all his goals. The second one, verses 29-30, doesn't go well at all because he is thwarted by ships from the west.

Frustrated by that setback, he turns his full fury against Jerusalem and the Temple. This is what verses 30-35 are all about. Judea and Jerusalem have already suffered from their unfortunate location: they lie squarely between Syria and Egypt and therefore armies have continually bulldozed through their land. They have been occupied by either north or south for the whole of this period. Now, they are firmly in the grip of the north, and this king makes it his business to crush them – specifically, to crush their religion. That is what Daniel prophesies: let's see how the rule of Antiochus IV played out in history.

The career of Antiochus Epiphanes

This king Antiochus IV is not the rightful heir to the throne – that would be his nephew Demetrius – but in the year 175 he seizes power anyway. He is extremely proud and arrogant, and he takes the title Antiochus Epiphanes, which is how he's usually known and makes it easier to pick him out from all the other kings named Antiochus. *Epiphanes* means 'God manifest'. In other words, he is claiming to be one of the gods. In the coins of the period, he has himself depicted with a star over his head and with the features of Zeus, the chief of the gods of Greece.

His subjects, in fact, aren't very impressed by this, and instead of *Epiphanes* they take to calling him *Epimanes*, which means madman – behind his back, obviously! The 'prince of the covenant' in verse 22 is probably the High Priest Onias III, who is deposed in the year 175 and later murdered.

But on his second invasion of Egypt, described in verses 29-30, Antiochus meets his match. The Romans show up. Their fleet brings one Gaius Popilius Laenas to the party; and he demands, on the authority of the Roman Senate, that Antiochus immediately withdraws from the country. Antiochus plays for time and says, I'd like a while to think about that. On that, Popilius takes a stick, draws a circle in the sand around Antiochus' feet, and says, You're going to give me a decision before you step out of that circle. Antiochus is cut down to size, and this spells the end of his ambitions to build his empire.

He is furious, verse 30. The following year, 167 BC, he turns his rage against the people of God in Judea. We have a vivid account of what happens next in the book called 1 Maccabees, which was written soon after the event. It's not in the Bible: it's part of what is called the Apocrypha, but it's generally regarded as a very good historical source. It tells the story of Antiochus and the Maccabean revolt against him; and this is a passage from near the beginning:

[54] Now on the fifteenth day of Chislev, in the one hundred and forty-fifth year, they erected a desolating sacrilege on the altar of burnt-offering. They also built altars in the surrounding towns of Judah, [55] and offered incense at the doors of the houses and in the streets. [56] The books of the law that they found they tore to pieces and burned with fire. [57] Anyone found possessing the book of the covenant, or anyone who adhered to the law, was condemned to death by decree of the king. [58] They kept using violence against Israel, against those who were found month after month in the towns. [59] On the twenty-fifth day of the month they offered sacrifice on the altar that was on top of the altar of burnt-offering. [60] In accordance with the decree, they put to death the women who had their children circumcised, [61] and

their families and those who circumcised them; and they hung the infants from their mothers' necks.

[62] But many in Israel stood firm and were resolved in their hearts not to eat unclean food. [63] They chose to die rather than to be defiled by food or to profane the holy covenant; and they did die. [64] Very great wrath came upon Israel.

(1 Maccabees 1:54-64, NRSV)

That simple, calm statement, 'and they did die', powerfully reflects the brave heroism of the resistance to Antiochus' rule. I have given a little more background about the Maccabean revolt in Appendix 3.

So Antiochus unleashes a reign of terror against the Jews. He bans circumcision, owning biblical scrolls, observing the Sabbath, all on pain of death; and he desecrates the Temple, halting the daily sacrifices and instead offering pigs and other unclean animals on the altar – the abomination mentioned in verse 31. This is unprecedented persecution that aims at nothing less than eradicating the Jewish faith. If he had succeeded, there would have been no Jewish environment for Jesus to be born into: no synagogues, no Temple, no scrolls for him to read; no knowledge of God's Law.

And as Daniel says in verse 32, some of the Jews go along with it. Antiochus successfully corrupts some of them. But others rebel – some with violence, including the Maccabees – others more peacefully. In these verses he talks about 'the wise', who remain faithful and instruct the others. The reference in verse 34 to 'receiving a little help' is usually thought to refer to the Maccabean revolt, which is otherwise not referred to in this chapter. In the end, history tells us, Antiochus' prohibition on Judaism is broken by the rebels, and the Temple is restored and rededicated. This is the event that Jews commemorate at the festival of Hanukkah to this day.

The king and his proud methods

Verses 36-39 move away from describing specific events to give us a sketch of the pride and the methods of the king. The only god he honours is a god of fortresses. Probably, that simply means that he worships military power. The strange reference in verse 37 to one whom women desire is probably a description of Tammuz, one of the Canaanite gods referred to in Ezekiel 8:14[15]. For all practical purposes, Antiochus is an atheist – just as Machiavelli would recommend. We will return to this portrait of rulers like Antiochus shortly.

The end of the king's career

In verses 40-44, the chapter gets really tricky – if it wasn't already! Who are these verses talking about? You see, there's a problem. History gives us four accounts of the closing years of Antiochus Epiphanes. They have their differences, but they all agree on the main points – and they bear no relation to what it says in these verses. According to history, Antiochus does none of this. Instead, he invades Persia, he tries to rob a temple, and he meets an untimely death nowhere near Jerusalem.

So either all the histories are wrong, which is possible, or else Daniel is now talking about someone else. Not Antiochus, but someone or something outside of history. This discrepancy raises an important question which we looked at in the Introduction: When was all this written? As I explained there, most recent commentators think that these chapters of Daniel were actually written during the time of Antiochus, and not back in the sixth century at all. I

---

[15] Tammuz was celebrated in an annual ritual which commemorated her mythological death. Another possibility here is the god Dionysius.

have set out why I think that view is mistaken, so do refer back to the Introduction if you'd like to! I believe there is a much better way to make sense of these difficult verses.

We can do that in the following way. There's a clear break in the progress of the text after verse 35. Verses 36-39 summarise the way that the evil king goes about his business, and it begins to stretch or exaggerate what Antiochus actually did. It's a bit like what David does in the Psalms, where you find yourself wondering sometimes,

---

Additional note: What happened to Antiochus?

History has left us with four accounts of the end of Antiochus Epiphanes. Three of these are found in the books of the Maccabees; one comes from Polybius, a Greek historian from the second century BC. Briefly, here are the options.

1. From 1 Maccabees 6: Antiochus attempts to rob a temple in Persia, but local people prevent this. Depressed by this and other bad news, Antiochus becomes depressed. In the end he realises that his impending death is due to his robbing the Temple in Jerusalem.
2. From 2 Maccabees 1: Antiochus was tricked and killed while in the act of robbing a temple in Persia.
3. From 2 Maccabees 9: following the failure to rob Persian temples and other bad news, Antiochus rages against and threatens the Jews. He is then struck by God with a painful disease and repents on his deathbed.
4. Polybius records that Antiochus was thwarted in an attempt to plunder a Persian temple, retreats and (still in Persia) is struck with madness and dies.

Clearly, these accounts have quite a lot in common and can largely be reconciled with one another. But none bears any relation to the closing section of Daniel 11.

Can he really be talking about himself here? He seems to be claiming so much for himself.

In the Psalms, that's because David is pointing forward to a greater David, a greater fulfilment, a perfect king, whom we know as Jesus Christ. The Lord Jesus is there in the background. This text is rather like that – but in the opposite direction! It starts with Antiochus, but then it 'lifts off' from talking just about him. There is someone or something greater and even more terrible than Antiochus lurking horribly in the background. When we get on to verses 40-44, Antiochus has been left behind completely.

These final verses include some notable connections with other events of the Old Testament. Verse 44 sounds like the story of Sennacherib in 2 Kings 19 and Isaiah 37. In verse 41, the nations that are spared by the evil king are the same ones that sided with Babylon when Judah was destroyed and exiled – and Ezekiel 25 talks about that. The idea is that they will 'be delivered from his hand' because they are already on the side of the power of evil. Libya and Cush in verse 43 represent the ends of the known world beyond Egypt: the conquest is being described in terms of the greatest possible extremes.

The story that is told here is a composite picture of all-out conflict, ruthless, far-reaching conquest and godless oppression; and it ends up with the evil power camping himself squarely on the holy city, Jerusalem or Mount Zion (verse 45a). It goes beyond Antiochus to a picture of what future tyrants – and perhaps one supreme, end-times antichrist – will do to God's people. And in the end, verse 45b, yes – they will meet their end. God will make sure of that.

This approach does not answer every question about the closing paragraph of the chapter. But I believe this is how Daniel 11 makes good sense for then and for now. As we will see, this perspective will help us to make the best sense of chapter 12 as well. Now let's see what this chapter can teach us about the world of today.

Godless power is futile

Glance back over verses 2-20. You might ask, Why are these verses here? Why not simply jump forward to Antiochus? This king, that king, this battle, that battle – it's a pattern of men rising to power, apparently being strong, and then rapidly falling again, time after time. And that's the point. See how often those words 'arise', 'be strong' and 'shall not stand' appear. Actually, every time the word 'but' or 'yet' appears in these verses, it's a signal that someone's plans have failed and got nowhere. Verses 9-12 provide some good examples of these reverses, and the pattern continues.

The message of this passage is that godless power is futile. These proud kings rise and fall so quickly. To quote the poet Thomas Gray, *The paths of glory lead but to the grave*[16]. Without God, it's all futility. The rise and fall of governments should not surprise us, nor the speed with which they fall. We can't pin our hopes on any government – nor on any other government we might prefer to see! – but only on the Lord.

Godless power is evil

Scattered through this long account is the expression 'do as he pleases' – verses 3, 16 and 36. Earthly rulers and powerful people, by and large, do as they please, and what they please is generally evil. Machiavelli was right. Here in

---

[16] From Gray's *Elegy in a country churchyard*. This verse was famously quoted by General James Wolfe on his way to assault Quebec in 1759 during the Seven Years' War between Britain and France. Wolfe remarked that 'I would rather be the author of that poem than take Quebec'. He died in the ensuing battle, underlining the truth of the words he had quoted.

this chapter, for instance, we find mass slaughter in verse 12 – passed over in a few words because it's not so unusual; devious manipulation in verse 17; ruthless invasions in every other verse; diplomatic deceit in verse 27. What a vivid and brutal depiction of international diplomacy!

Human power is not always as bad as that; and it's nearly always better to have a bad government than no government at all. But often it is that bad. And great outbreaks of evil should not surprise us. History is full of it; so is the world of today. Of course, not all godless power is in governments. We think, for example, of the cold and ruthless outrages of IS, seen in incidents like the slaughter of hundreds of people in a mosque in Egypt, merely because they were supposedly the wrong kind of Muslim. It's right to be horrified, but we shouldn't be surprised.

Godless power is hostile

Look at verses 30-33 and think about that extract from 1 Maccabees. Antiochus displays unprecedented fury as he tries to stamp out the true religion. But it didn't start with him, and it doesn't end with him. Already in verse 16 there's a reference to destruction in 'the beautiful land' – the land of Israel. Then look at verses 36-39. It's a portrait of the tyrant in every age who hates God's people. He is selfish, self-promoting, blasphemous, manipulative. He uses religion for his own end, carves up the land for his followers, and for a time, he is successful.

No, Antiochus is not the end of this. You can find a very similar picture in Revelation 13:1-10. It's the passage about the Beast that we referenced from Daniel 7 – the Beast who does just what we find here. This is godless power, turned against the people of God – turned against us and our family in other places. Persecution of the Church of Jesus Christ is normal. It should not surprise us, and a passage like this helps us to be prepared.

Godless power is directed

All through the story of Antiochus there are markers of God's sovereignty, like little flags in the text. See the end of verse 24, for instance, with its note about the brevity of his triumphs. It's a hint that someone else is really in charge. Or verse 27, which notes that an end is in view and there is a limit to his success. Someone has appointed an end to his antics – and we know who that someone is! There are similar notes in verses 35 and 36.

Perhaps most comforting is the line in verse 36 about the completion of the time of wrath (or fury). Whether we take this to refer to the king's fury against his enemies or the wrath of God in judgement, the point is that there is a limited time for these events to occur and to conclude. And the limit is set not by Antiochus and his ilk, but by the Lord.

God is in control, as we see set out beautifully in Psalm 75:3-7. That's the truth behind all the arrogance and ambition in this chapter, all the rising and falling of kings and princes. Their godless power is given by the Lord, managed by the Lord, directed by the Lord. Knowing that should give us great confidence.

Again, we might ask why the Bible gives such minute detail of a man like Antiochus, who frankly most of us hadn't heard of and who has long since faded into the mists of the distant past. One reason, especially for the Jews, is this. Daniel is writing as an exile. The Exile took place as a punishment for the people's sin and rebellion. The Law warned them about it; the prophets told them it would happen if they did not repent and turn back to the Lord. But they didn't, so the Exile came as promised. It was deserved; it was obviously under God's control; and in the end, the people understood that.

But this time is going to be different. Antiochus is directly attacking God's faithful people with every intention of destroying their religion. This is worse than the Babylonians ever did. And yet, they are not guilty of outright rebellion against God. They have done nothing especially bad to deserve all this – the crazy megalomaniac and his brutality, personally directed against God's people and the holy covenant, this bitter suffering that is not a punishment for their sin.

This is new, and Daniel 11 gives them due warning that it will happen. It would show the Jews of those days, and it shows us today, that God is in control even when things happen that we cannot understand, that fit no known pattern, that just seem blatantly wrong. We need that reassurance, and this chapter provides it. Whatever comes against us, whatever trials we face, all is directed by a God who loves us and wants our best. And that leads on to the final point.

Godless power is purposeful

Yes, godless power is futile, because it never gets anywhere. But on another level, it is purposeful. Look at verse 35. The 'wise' here are the people who are godly, who are faithful, who understand how the Lord wants them to live. These verses describe how they will suffer at the hands of Antiochus. The key words are *so that*. Those are wonderful words, because they tell us there is a purpose. There is a point to the suffering. It's *so that* they may be purified, refined and made spotless, through what they suffer.

Here we find another reason for the detailed account in this chapter. In the first half of Daniel, God always seems to rescue the people who are faithful to him. It may be terrifying for a while – think fiery furnace, think lions' den – but the Lord always seems to step in to rescue. The

88

second half of the book tells a different story. It won't always be like that. Sometimes, the trial leads to death. Sometimes, the fire will burn, the lions will bite. We don't know how our trials will turn out; we don't know how tough they will get.

But we do know there is a 'so that'. Look at 1 Peter 1:6-9, which we could call the New Testament equivalent of that verse in Daniel. Notice the 'so that' in verse 7. Trials will come – all kinds of them. Some trials come just because we live in a broken world. We get ill, we see our loved ones suffer, we have to face our own decline and death. Some, because we are Christians – persecution, abuse, all the cost of faithfully following Christ day by day.

But in the Lord's hands, there is always a 'so that'. Through these trials, the genuineness of our faith is proved. We find out, and others can clearly see, that what we have believed is real! That it works, and that it's true! And Jesus Christ gets honored and praised. Through trials, we get more love, and more joy, and we look forward more and more to seeing him face to face when our salvation is complete. That's the 'so that'.

What a world we live in! It's a world that so often is evil, hostile to believers; that so often seems utterly futile. Yet all that we see out there, and all that we experience in ourselves, is in the Lord's hands. It is directed and overseen by him. So let's trust him for that.

Questions to discuss or think about

1. How did you react when you first read this chapter? Do you agree that it has a lot to teach us about godless power and the hope that we have in Christ?

2. What do you feel when you hear news of terrorist outrages or massacres? How does this chapter help us not to be shaken by such news?

3. In your own life, where do you find it hardest to believe that the Lord is working out his purposes for your good and his glory? How can you be praying about that now?

Daniel 12: The end will come

Everyone loves a happy ending! Not every story actually has one, but we warm to those that do. Whether it's *Pride and Prejudice*, *Lord of the Rings* or *Star Wars*, or even that post-modern identity fable *Frozen*, we love to see our heroes battling through against all kinds of obstacles to triumph in the end. The obstacles may take the shape of family opinion, or thousands of sword-wielding orcs, or stormtroopers with ray guns: struggles there always are, but vindication comes in the end.

But what happens when you are in the story yourself? How do you know whether your own story is going to have a happy ending or not? There's a great passage in *Lord of the Rings* where Sam muses about this with Frodo, thinking about the great stories of the past and then realizing that they are in a great story themselves. 'I wonder what sort of a tale we've fallen into?', says Sam. 'I wonder', says Frodo. 'But I don't know. And that's the way of a real tale. Take any one that you're fond of. You may know, or guess, what kind of a tale it is, happy-ending or sad-ending, but the people in it don't know. And you don't want them to.'

What about the real world? What about our shared story as God's people? We know there are all kinds of struggles and conflicts in this life – physical, emotional and spiritual battles – so can we know that *our* story has a happy ending? And *how* do we know? Then, supposing we do know the story's ending, will we make it through to the end? If so, what are we supposed to do while we are waiting for the end? Those are exactly the questions that Daniel 12 can tell us. In this closing chapter, we get to hear about the ending to our story. And we are told what to do while we wait for the credits to roll.

We are in the final section of the final vision. This is the vision that began in chapter 10, where a fearsome angelic figure, the mysterious man in linen, appears and prepares Daniel to receive the message. Chapter 11 has dwelt on an evil king who would appear long after Daniel's time. History revealed him to be Antiochus Epiphanes, a monstrous persecutor of God's people. We saw that verses 21-35 focus directly on the career of this Antiochus. Then towards the end of the chapter, the scene shifts. We lift off from the story of Antiochus to a summary of the violence and troubles of the end times. What is described in the closing verses of chapter 11 does not describe the historical Antiochus. Instead, we are given a composite picture of persecution of God's people, ending with a direct assault on Jerusalem, the holy city.

So as we enter chapter 12 – remembering these chapter divisions aren't part of the text and they often appear in the wrong places – we will not expect that the events described here relate to the time of Antiochus. They will be looking further forward than that, and so it proves. We are looking here at the end of this world's story and also the end of our own story.

Overview of the vision

Verses 1-4, then, complete the main message delivered by 'the man dressed in linen'. These verses contain a highly compressed summary of the key events of the end times – the times in which we are living today. Straight away, we meet once more the archangel Michael, who has special responsibility for looking after the people of God (verse 1). We're told he will arise. The next few verses show that this is a time of great suffering, but also a time of judgement and salvation. It is in this context that Michael takes action.

There is one other biblical reference that can tell us what that action is, and it comes in Revelation 12:7-9 (which we have already referenced from Daniel 10). Michael and his angelic crew are here to be seen taking hold of Satan and throwing him out of heaven. From the rest of Revelation 12 we can see that this event is connected with Jesus Christ and his death on the cross. As that shattering event takes place on earth, Satan is expelled from heaven by Michael. His power is broken by what Jesus has done in our world below.

Satan is thrown down, and Revelation 12 goes on to warn us that this will lead to greater troubles here on earth, as Satan charges off in hot pursuit of God's people. That is just what Daniel 12:1 warns of too. From the time of Jesus' ministry through to his second coming, Satan is on the rampage here on earth – but not for ever. Still in verse 1, we are promised that everyone whose name is found in the book will be delivered.

Verse 2 looks forward to resurrection. This is a wonderful verse. It's the clearest statement of the resurrection anywhere in the Old Testament. The dead will rise to life. The division hinted at in verse 1 (some will be delivered, therefore some will not) is emphasised here. Some will go to everlasting life; some will go to everlasting shame. The passage doesn't use the actual words, but this is a one-line description of heaven and hell. The Lord Jesus picks up this verse in John 5:28-29 – the Bible speaks with one voice about eternity. That's the ending: a happy ending, or a sad one.

Then verses 3-4 talk about life now, life in the waiting time. We'll come back to verse 3, but in verse 4 Daniel is told to seal up the message until the time of the end. It doesn't mean he has to keep it secret – otherwise we wouldn't have it in our hands now! It's a way of telling him that this message is not about his own time: it is to remain permanently in fixed form and cannot be tampered with, however far off the end may be. The whole narrative of chapter 11 and into chapter 12 is set in Daniel's future. Meanwhile, people will be running around seeking for knowledge, seeking enlightenment. Many of them will be looking in all the wrong places, just as we see today; but those who seek God's wisdom look in the right place, and they find it.

That brings to an end the message of the man in linen. We come to the concluding words of the book with some closing questions and answers, in the company of two additional figures (verses 5-6). We cannot identify these extra characters. Probably they are here as angelic witnesses to the dramatic oath that's about to be spoken. The Bible often features the idea of having two or three witnesses to confirm the truth of important events. The question is, How long until all these amazing events we've been hearing about are complete? Matters of judgement and salvation are certainly astonishing to angels, who unlike us have no personal experience of them.

It's that question 'How long' again – a question we heard from another angel in chapter 8, the question that is asked so often in the psalms and in Habakkuk, the question that even angels ask. How long before the time of suffering is over and we reach the happy ending?

The answer is both dramatic and mysterious, verse 7. In his answer, the man in linen gives a *time* period – hold on to that for now – and an *event*. The sign for the completion of this time period is the breaking of God's people. Perhaps not surprisingly, Daniel doesn't understand. He asks a question of his own (verse 8) – What will be the outcome of all this? The answer he is given is indirect. He is told to go his way, get on with his life; and then once more the division into two pathways is stressed, the righteous going this way and the wicked going that way.

Now we come to the very mysterious verses 11-12. These are very obscure verses, and before trying to explain them I want to be clear what this whole period of time represents. This chapter has very close links to several places in Revelation. In fact, it's good to read the second half of Daniel with the book of Revelation alongside. Revelation borrows extensively from the imagery of Daniel; and in return, Revelation fills out and explains some of the most baffling parts of Daniel.

If you have time, it would be good to read Revelation 10 and 11 at this point. Here is a quick summary. Revelation 10 features a mighty angel of dazzling appearance, who raises a hand to heaven and swears by Almighty God, and declares the imminent fulfilment of God's purposes. That already sounds familiar (glance back to Daniel 10:5-6 to remind yourself what the man in linen looks like). Then Revelation 11 describes a period of forty-two months, or 1260 days, during which God's people – symbolised by two witnesses, another possible link with the closing vision of Daniel – will speak powerfully for him, while the world opposes and hates them. At the end of that time, the church appears to be completely dead and destroyed for a brief time, before God steps in and raises them to life.

That quick summary should convince you that these passages in Daniel and Revelation are talking about the same thing. The time period in verse 7 has already appeared in Daniel 7:25. 'Time, times and half a time' – that's three and a half years or forty-two months, 1260 days. In Hebrew thinking, the year basically consisted of twelve months of thirty days. It is the same period as in Revelation, and it means the same thing.

As we've said before, it is a symbolic period, the time period from Christ's first coming to his second coming, what we call the 'church age', the time we are living in now. At the end of that time, persecution of the Church gets so severe that for a while, it looks as though the Church – the holy people – is dead. Exactly what Daniel is being told here in verse 7. So that's the 1260 days, and that's what happens at the end of it. I think that is clear enough. The really tricky part is the additional numbers in verses 11-12. The commentators give up hope at this point! All kinds of ideas have been tried out to explain the 1290 and the 1335 days – see the additional note.

My view is that we have to start by saying that this 1260 day period is the one that we *do* understand and is used elsewhere in Daniel and Revelation. So that's the basis, and then we see that the other numbers are small additions to the 1260. My own thought is set out in the figure below.

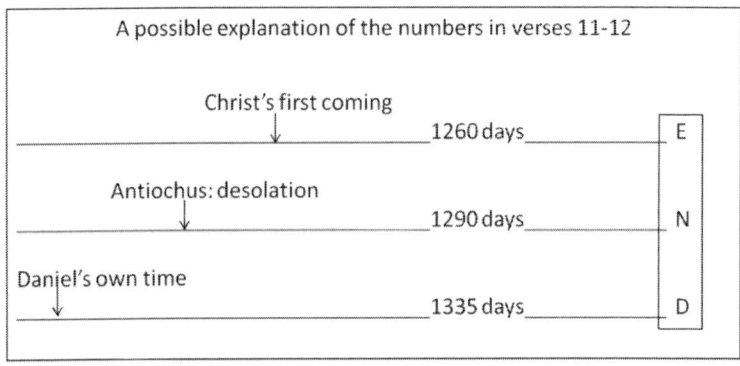

A possible explanation of the numbers in verses 11-12

Christ's first coming
1260 days   E

Antiochus: desolation
1290 days   N

Daniel's own time
1335 days   D

Additional note: the extra days

Commentators have struggled to explain the numbers in verses 11-12. Most of the recent explanations assume the author is referring to the persecution by Antiochus and is writing at that time. That is not the approach I am taking.

Perhaps the strangest idea connects these verses with the 1150 days in chapter 8, which clearly do refer to the actions of Antiochus. Apparently, the writer thought that the defilement of the Temple would last 1150 days, but he got it a bit wrong. When Antiochus isn't finished after 1150 days, the author adds a bigger number at the end – but without deleting the 1150. Then, when 1290 days still isn't enough, he adds on a few more to make 1335!

Ernest Lucas sets out four possibilities that have been suggested, including this one. The others are:

1. The numbers represent three different pairs of significant events during Antiochus' persecution and its aftermath.

2. Different calendars have been used to reckon the three and a half year period, resulting in different totals of days.

3. Some lost, symbolic meaning.

The last of these is possible: the others do not stand up to scrutiny.

1260 days correspond to the time from Christ's first coming to his second, as we've said. But you see that verse 11 starts its count further back, from the actions of Antiochus in the Jerusalem Temple, which we know took place in the 160s BC. For the second time in this vision, we read of the abomination in the Temple. That gives us a slightly longer period to the end – call it symbolically an extra month, so 1290 days in all. But then Daniel himself stands at around 537 BC, so the total time for God's people to endure is longer again – call it an extra month and a half, so 1335 days as a grand total. From where you are *now*, Daniel, there are 1335 days for God's people to stand firm.

That's the best I can do with the numbers. Sometimes we have to admit, We just don't know! Let's not be sidetracked by that, though. The text doesn't make much of the numbers, so neither should we! The main point is, all this assures us of the ending, if we can get there. The ending for God's people is resurrection and eternal life – so never mind the numbers, let's rejoice in that!

And meanwhile, here and now, what does God's Word call us to do? What is Daniel told, twice in these closing verses? Very simply, to go his way. Don't obsess about the end times. Don't try counting the dates and figuring out the numbers. Don't drop what you are doing, just keep going. And as you do that, and as you wait for the ending to unfold and the final credits to roll, here are three very simple commands for us to hear.

Trust

We need to trust and be saved. Look at verses 1b-2 again. There is a happy ending here – but not for everyone. It is only for those included in the people of God, only for those whose names are found written in the book of life. We need to go to Revelation again, where this judgement scene is filled out. In Revelation 20:11-15, the resurrection has happened, and everyone stands before God to be judged. What we need on that day is for our names to be written in the book of life. Without that, we cannot be saved, or spared from the lake of fire that is eternal hell. There is only one way of escape, and that is to trust in Jesus Christ.

Then, we are called to trust that all this will happen. Look at verse 7. Raising *one* hand towards heaven was a common way of reinforcing an oath. This angel raises *both* hands and swears in the name of the Lord God Almighty, making it the most powerful statement it is possible for any being in heaven or on earth to give. This powerful emphasis – along with the appearance of two extra witnesses – is for Daniel's benefit and ours, to reassure us that these things will actually happen in the way God's Word tells us.

God's promise of resurrection is true. Death is not the end – let's trust him for it! God's promise of eternity is true. We will live for ever in the heavenly city in the constant presence of Jesus Christ, our Saviour, our Husband, and our King. Let's trust him for it! The time of suffering may seem long, but it is limited.

Let's determine that we will believe and embrace these wonderful truths, whatever happens. Let's rest in knowing that. Verse 13 tells Daniel he will rest, after death, but the rest starts now in the sense that we have the peace and security of knowing God's promises are true. Jesus has won, and he's preparing a place for us now.

Shine

Look at verse 3. We came across these wise people in 11:33-35 where they were instructing others, helping them to stand firm in a time of terrible, life-threatening trial. The two halves of this verse are parallel: the wise are the same as those who lead people to righteousness. It's what they do. 'Wise' docs not mean intelligent. In the Bible, being wise or foolish has nothing whatever to do with what we call intelligent. Wisdom in the Bible is a moral term: it means following the patterns and ways of life that God has designed us for. This is what we are called to.

Think of what Paul says in Philippians 2:14-16. We live in a dark world: Daniel has told us about that in the most vivid terms. And as God's people, we are to *shine* among the people of this world, as we hold on firmly to God's promises and hold out the message of life. Shine out brilliantly now, like a star on a deep, dark night, and you will shine out brilliantly for ever and ever. It's our life, our purity, our witness, for others to see; it's our words, for others to know.

Persevere

Look at verse 12. Whatever the 1335 days means exactly, the thrust of this verse is obvious. The blessing of life, eternal, glorious life, is for those who persevere to the end. Yes, the times will be hard. Yes, this life brings trials and suffering and persecution. But there is a purpose to it all, verse 10. The words about being refined and purified echo 11:35. The words 'so that' are not used this time, but the meaning is the same. In God's plans, there is always a 'so that'. As we experience the trials of this life, we are being purified, refined – like steel in a blast furnace, or like silver or gold melted in the crucible. Knowing that purpose will help us to persevere.

We know that if we are true believers, the Lord *will* keep us. We *don't* lose our salvation. We *will* persevere. But the Bible still encourages us to keep examining ourselves to make sure of where we stand (2 Corinthians 13:5-6). We must still choose to persevere. Let's keep going, then, because of Jesus Christ and all that lies ahead of us.

Like Daniel, we don't understand everything. Even at the end of the book, he doesn't understand it all. That's OK. We simply need to dwell on what we do know and understand.

Think of it this way. The whole book of Daniel is the story of how God vindicates his own true people. In the first half of the book, he generally does that at once. Daniel and friends choose a thin vegetarian diet – and immediately, they thrive! The three friends get dropped into a furnace – and they survive unscathed! Daniel prophesies the fall of the kingdom – and it falls that very night! He is locked into the lions' den, and they don't even growl at him! God's people are vindicated. They win the day. Sometimes, God does that for us at once.

But sometimes, it's not like that. Sometimes, in fact, we simply continue to suffer, we remain in the place of trial, right through life and into death. That's what we see in the second half of Daniel. But that vindication, that rescue, is just as real and just as certain when it comes after death. One day, everyone will be raised to life; and then perfect justice will be done. And God's people will be eternally vindicated, eternally declared in the right.

Persecuted believers have often drawn great strength from the book of Daniel. The Anabaptists, persecuted by both Catholics and mainstream Protestants in the sixteenth century, quoted from it more often than any other book of the Bible in the midst of their struggles. They looked to the courage of Daniel and his three friends in the face of death (chapters 3 and 6) and to the promise in chapter 12 that they would be delivered through death[17]. The promises are for us too. The Lord is faithful. He will take us through death to a glorious resurrection, and eternity with him. Because of Jesus Christ, we *will* make it through to the end of the story.

---

[17] See Lucas, *Daniel*, p.305.

Questions to discuss or think about

1. How does this chapter help us to trust more firmly in God's promises about the future?

2. Think about the places where you spend your daily life (home, workplace, study, social life and so on). Where do you find it hardest to 'shine like stars'? Why do you think that is? Have you found any encouragement here?

3. Do you believe that the Lord will keep you safe to the end, whatever life looks like in the meantime? What makes it hard to believe at times, and how can the book of Daniel help?

Appendix 1
The Son of Man and the holy ones of the Most High

Chapter 7 is complicated, not in its core message but in its structure. There is a lot of interpretation going on, and some of it is repeated. Something that is not directly interpreted is the figure of the 'son of man'. There has been a lot of scholarly debate around who or what this figure represents and how he relates to the 'holy ones of the Most High' (the literal translation of verse 18). We need to understand who they are, too.

In chapter 7 we encounter the Son of Man just once (verses 13-14) and the holy ones of the Most High five times (verses 18, 21, 22, 25, 27). In verse 18 they are said to receive the kingdom and to possess it for ever; in verses 21-22 they are assaulted by the 'little horn' until they receive the Kingdom; in verse 25 we are given more detail about the oppression they suffer; and finally in verse 27 the verdict of verse 18 is repeated and expanded.

Who are these holy people? The Aramaic text simply calls them 'holy ones' and some commentators think they are actually angels. That idea doesn't make a lot of sense, however, especially as it is hard to see how the 'little horn', which definitely represents a human being, could oppress (literally 'wear away' or 'harass') angels (verse 25)! No, the holy ones are definitely people. But which people are they? It's unlikely that they represent the whole nation of Israel. Daniel himself will confess the extreme un-holiness of his people in chapter 9. Rather, we should think of the true people of God, a faithful remnant at the heart of Israel. They will endure bitter suffering at the hands of a human tyrant (verses 21, 25) but ultimately will be vindicated by

God himself (verses 18, 22, 27). And that interpretation allows us to identify them with the people of God down to the present day, members of the new humanity in Christ drawn from both Jews and Gentiles, described by Paul in Ephesians 2:11-22.

What about the Son of Man? Why do we identify this mysterious figure with Jesus Christ, given that 'son of man' can mean simply 'a member of the human race'? Here are three reasons, which were summarised in the main text.

1. the 'son of man' figure comes with the clouds of heaven: this is the language of theophany, the way that God is described in the narrative of Sinai, at many other points elsewhere in the Exodus narratives and frequently in Kings, Chronicles and in the Psalms and prophets. The figure therefore has both human and god-like attributes.

2. The 'son of man' is given an eternal and indestructible kingdom and is made the focus of the worship of all nations. The New Testament makes it clear that it is Jesus Christ who fits this description. And only God himself is worthy of such worship.

3. Jesus himself adopted the name Son of Man for himself. His intention was to convey something like 'the perfect representative of the human race', but the connection to Daniel 7 is obvious.

The alternative suggested by some commentators, that the 'son of man' is merely a symbol for divine rule, makes little sense. A symbol cannot have an encounter with a person (the Ancient of Days), be led, or receive a kingdom. Scarcely better, for similar reasons, is the suggestion that he is a corporate representation of the people of the Most High. We have to understand him as a specific individual.

What of the character of his kingdom? We should not miss the sharp contrast between the kingdoms of the beasts, which are distorted, evil and sub-human, and the perfect humanity seen in the God-given kingdom of the Son of Man.

It is also interesting to see that there are connections with King David. In Psalm 89, David appears in a role which seems to prefigure the Son of Man in Daniel 7. The similarities are significant: he does not *take* the kingdom, it is *given* to him by God; the kingdom is described as everlasting; and the royal oracle in Psalm 89 is given 'in a vision to your faithful people' (verse 19). And Jesus Christ is of course the descendant of King David, and the one who fulfils all the kingly promises made of him.

What, then, is the connection between the Son of Man and the holy people? Both are said to receive the kingdom after the destruction of the fourth beast. The same court that awards the Son of Man his kingdom (verses 9-14) strips the holy people's oppressor of his power and gives the kingdom to *them*. The Son of Man, then, is the *representative* and *leader* of the holy people. In Daniel 7, they suffer oppression and temporary defeat. That points us to the fact that their representative would do the same. It is through the suffering, death and resurrection of the Lord Jesus Christ that victory is won and the everlasting kingdom is secured.

Appendix 2
The 'seventy sevens'

The view on the meaning of the 'seventy sevens' at the end of chapter 9 that is laid out in the main text is my own, but it differs only in detail from that held by a number of commentators. There is one very significant alternative view, which is the one held by dispensationalists. This would be regarded as the standard position among many evangelicals, especially in the USA.

On the dispensationalist view, the seventieth 'week' represents a period of tribulation lasting seven years, immediately before the final return of Jesus Christ. Usually this is described as the Great Tribulation. These seven years include the seven seals, the seven trumpets and the seven bowls of Revelation. During the first part of the Tribulation, the Antichrist arises and makes a covenant with Israel (note that this view also believes in the separate identity of the nation of Israel from the Church of Jesus Christ). At the mid-point of the seven years, however, he breaks the covenant and this leads to worldwide persecution of the Jews.

People who subscribe to this view will generally also hold that the first sixty-nine 'sevens' also represent a literal period of time – 483 years. This will be fitted to the number of years from some event at the end of the Exile through to the life of Christ. A key part of this view, therefore, is that there is a very long gap between the end of 'week sixty-nine' and the beginning of the still future 'week seventy'. It is not too strong to say that this understanding of the seventy 'sevens' is foundational to the whole dispensational scheme of the end times.

A few comments on the dispensational view, which will explain why I don't accept it:

1. There is no hint in Daniel of the required gap between week sixty-nine and week seventy.

2. There is no obvious reason why Daniel should have been given a detailed timetable of events thousands of years ahead of his own time, especially as this would not fit into the context of the rest of Daniel 7-12 which is concerned with the time running through to the first coming of Christ.

3. There is no satisfactory way of fitting 483 years (seven times sixty-nine) to the period between any significant date and either the birth or death of Christ. The one that comes nearest involves Nehemiah's commission from Artaxerxes in 444 BC and the death of Jesus in 32 AD (given that the 'years' are of 360 days, whereas our dates use solar years). However, both these dates are almost certainly wrong, and anyway it was not Artaxerxes who gave orders for the rebuilding of Jerusalem.

4. As many have noted, dispensational theology is not very sensitive to biblical genre. This means that apocalyptic writing tends to get interpreted too literally, leaving little room for the use of symbolic numbers etc. Indeed, dispensationalists often do not recognise apocalyptic as a separate genre.

For further illustration of this, see my commentary on Revelation, *The Final Word*. Particularly helpful on the dispensational view of Daniel 9 is Sam Storms' *Kingdom Come: the amillennial alternative* – though I don't agree with him on everything!

If you have been taught the dispensational view of Daniel 9, I would encourage you to consider these points.

Appendix 3
The Maccabees

In December 167 BC, pagan sacrifice was offered in the Temple and the great persecution of the Jews began. Representatives of the government travelled through the land to enforce the new decrees prohibiting Jewish practices. When they came to the village of Modin, they tried to persuade the local priest Mattathias to sacrifice to pagan gods. Mattathias refused to do so, and killed both a compliant Jew and a royal official. Along with his sons, he then took to the Judean hills and raised a revolt.

Mattathias died a year or two later, passing the leadership to his son Judas. 'Maccabee', probably meaning 'hammer', was his nickname, and the whole movement became known colloquially as the Maccabees. They used violent guerrilla tactics against the regime of Antiochus and its sympathisers. Among other actions, they destroyed pagan altars and forcibly circumcised children. At first, they refused to fight on the Sabbath, but that tactic changed after a number of faithful Jews were killed on that day. Pious Jews generally supported the Maccabees in what they regarded as a holy war.

Judas' tactics were successful and he won repeated victories against Seleucid troops. Eventually in 165 or 164, Antiochus withdrew the ban on the Jewish religion, though he retained his grip on Jerusalem and the high priesthood. Judas was able to move his forces into Jerusalem and rededicate the Temple. The desecrated altar of burnt offering was removed and its stones placed 'in a convenient place on the Temple hill until a prophet should come to tell what to do with them' (1 Maccabees 4:46, NRSV). This note is highly significant, as it shows the Jews of this period were well aware that prophecy had ceased. A new altar was set up and sacrifices resumed in December 164.

Further struggles were to follow, even though Antiochus

Epiphanes died in 163. Judas himself was killed in battle against the Syrian army in 160, but his brother Jonathan pursued the fight, as did the last of the brothers, Simon, into the 140s. At last in 142, Judea secured effective independence from the Seleucid empire. A new dynasty of kings (the Hasmoneans, after Hashmon, an ancestor of Mattathias) was established. It ruled with varying degrees of effectiveness until the Romans arrived in 63 BC. By the time of Jesus' ministry, Judean independence was a distant memory.

.

23916361R00065

Printed in Poland
by Amazon Fulfillment
Poland Sp. z o.o., Wrocław